"I recommend *Creating the Reflecti[ve ...]*  coaching practitioner who, pausin[g ...] wonders where to begin. Start here!

This practical book takes me on a [...] diverse ways I can enter reflection, a[nd ...] my own approach:

- gentle encouragement to experiment with processing styles outside my usual preference
- the invitation to put aside a space each month for reflection appeals to my way of working
- the myriad ways to reflect, laid out for me to choose from is tantalising
- repeated suggestions to 'use it, ignore it, adapt it... it is up to you' engage me in a nourishing experiment
- anecdotes from practitioners are true to life and the fact that reflection is rarely a straight-line experience from A to B!

I like the perfectly imperfect portrayals that mirror the reality of many client sessions, the scribbles, clunks, and distractions described alongside the a-ha moments and turning points. I feel reassured that some of my methods are similar and delighted by the breadth of innovative ideas. The chapter on theory is perhaps the best part of the book for supervisors. It brings together so much, and is written clearly, pragmatically and with sensitivity to the breadth of the coaching field.

I AM enjoying this book immensely. It is norm to write an endorsement in the past tense, but this is a resource that will keep on giving! Thanks to Michelle's work to bring great contributors from her extensive network, I am adding to the dimensions and refreshing the structure I use. It has really got me thinking and re-creating my reflective practice."

Lorenza Clifford, *Founding Director of Coachange.org and Current Chair of the Association of Coaching Supervisors, affectionately known as AOCS: Voice for coaching supervision and source of strong community for dialogue and developing our practice and profession*

"It is empirically evidenced that reflective practice is an excellent method of raising awareness, an essential attribute for coaches & mentors. In *Creating the Reflective Habit* Michelle provides an invaluable resource for coaches, mentors and anyone who recognises the value of taking a moment to pause. The content is awash with detail, information, and most importantly, exercises and activities that practitioners can use to maximise the benefit they gain from their own reflections. This is the absolute 'must' for transferring theory into action.

The layout of the book will appeal to 'dippers' like me. It provides the opportunity to read about the concept and then try different tools and techniques. The range is incredibly broad, and will no doubt introduce techniques that the reader may be unfamiliar with, such as Kwirkeez, Blob Trees or using music and poetry. This smorgasbord offers the opportunity to expand knowledge and experience and can only benefit those who are prepared to explore and develop their own reflective practices.

I will be recommending this book to all our members as well as using it as my own resource to enhance my reflective practice. I strongly recommend you do too."

David Monro-Jones, *Chief Operating Officer and Head of Accreditation, International Authority for Professional Coaching & Mentoring (IAPC&M)*

"Reflective practice is an integral and continuous part of our professional development as coaches, mentors, and supervisors. This scholarly book presents us with a rich source of knowledge, experience, and academic research. But more importantly, it challenges our perceptions of what reflective practice is or can be, and in turn offers us new and innovative ways to reinvigorate our learning. This book is a treasure trove of resources which will be revisited repeatedly by practitioners and supervisors alike; I will be one of them."

Rachael Hanley-Browne, *President, EMCC UK*

"Yet another triumph from Michelle who has brought together a mouth-watering array of approaches this time for independent reflection. She challenges the all too familiar assumption that reflection centres on written journalling. The book offers 60 prompts (yes 60!) leveraging the range of processing preferences, which include cognitive or thinking and writing exercises, but goes on to offer so much more, including poetry, visual, auditory, prompts – and my favourite, kinaesthetic. Looking at the index of the 60 prompts I wondered where I would start. However, Michelle had thought about that; she provides a 'how to' approach. As I read this chapter, I could almost hear her voice; warm, professional and pragmatic – it was like she was coaching me through my own experiment. I thoroughly enjoyed reading the theory chapter too. It began with more familiar material and then brought in new literature and research which really got my attention. This chapter will be a great primer for my students – giving them lots of ideas around what they might choose to reflect upon, and how they might organise their portfolio of reflective activities. It also offers two models that will help them map their journey as a reflective practitioner.

Although the book feels like it is written with coaches in mind, I can see myself offering many of the exercises to my executive clients. If anyone ever says to me that their reflective practice lacks inspiration, I will point them to this book. Once you've read *Creating the Reflective Habit*, you can never be short of ideas for creating breadth, depth, variety and a generous slice of playfulness to your reflective practice. No practitioner's bookshelf should be without it!"

Damian Goldvarg, *PhD, MCC, Principal of The Goldvarg Consulting Group, past ICF Global Chair 2013–2014*

"The honesty of this book is touching. The author shares her journey of her relationship with professional reflection, how it has challenged her and how she has leant into that challenge. In so doing, she has crafted this colourful, insightful book of that journey. She inquires into how reflection can be expressed and expounded in so many forms, in addition to a perhaps traditional method of journalling. She opens up a whole and, in many ways, magical landscape of how we might choose to reflect on ourselves, our clients and those 'moments' which help us create a shift in our practice.

There is encouragement to experiment with what might work for us, structuring the book into processing preferences and offering 12 templates each time – inspirational materials that we are invited to play with to see what works for us. I was captivated by the auditory chapter, so many soundscapes that tinkled with my curiosity – I can imagine using these to help me concentrate but also as catalysts to provoke a different rhythm of thinking about my relationships with my clients.

The creativity and range of the templates provided is striking and rich. I have already started to use them for my own reflection and will be offering them to my corporate clients and supervision clients alike. In a world in which I occasionally experience a crisis of time or energy and really need a reflective moment, I love the idea of opening this book at random to see what that template evokes for me.

In addition, there is a useful chapter which invites self-coaching, offering 7 aspects of developing a more reflective practice. Presented as a series of experiments, each one triggered a new experiment and reflective cycle, inspiring me to refresh my practice in small ways.

The final chapter is more theoretical, in which Michelle's narrative style helps to weave your way through the rigour of the literature, nudging you to consider the range of forms of expression of your reflective practice and how you might notice that practice maturing.

This is more than a book, it is a companion that will help to expand your reflective practices, ensuring greater depth of felt experience for the work and the enriching of your developmental narrative."

Frances White, *Global Organisational Coach & Supervisor, APECS Board Member & Master Coach*

"Professional reflective practice is such a fundamental building block of professional coaching – but how do we become good at it? This book offers us rich range of insight and resources to help us hone these skills, clearly written for the coach and supervisor, but has applications for leaders too.

What inspires me, in particular, is to see how many organisations are now integrating coaching into their cultural style, from when and we started the Association for Coaching, 2 decades ago. We encourage all organisations to build in the practices for their leaders to take time out to reflect, given the tendency for increasingly packed diaries and Zoom calls.

The book starts with a more theoretical chapter, synthesising some of the more familiar literature and introducing new models too. I particularly enjoyed how the author drew attention to how our reflection changes over time – inviting us to reflect before, during and after our client work. The second chapter takes us on a journey of experimentation, breaking down into 7 elements how we might go about building a new habit. This is easy to read and encouraging, and enables the reader to make the most of what follows.

The rest of the book has echoes of the editor's previous book (*101 Coaching Supervision Techniques, Approaches, Enquiries and Experiments*) in that each reflective prompt is clearly laid out and positioned as a 'pathway' that the reader can follow, meander from or indeed choose an entirely different route – the encouragement to experiment is clear. Each chapter prioritises a different processing style – a refreshing provocation that reflection isn't just about 'musing' or about 'journalling' – but a form of learning which is uniquely ours. Additionally, in this book, Michelle shares how she discovered the prompt and/or how it impacted on her – it feels very much as though she is accompanying the reader in a shared reflective discovery.

Perhaps ironically it was tricky to carve out the time to review the book! Yet having opened the cover it quickly engaged my senses to not just to read it, but to play with the vast array of prompts on offer. I can imagine some people will work methodically through, perhaps chapter by chapter or, sequentially through the series of 12 prompts across the chapters. Others may just dip in at random. I would encourage our members – coaches, supervisors and leaders to pick this book up and notice its potential for deepening their understanding of themselves and those they work with. Once picked up, I can attest that it will not be easy to put it down!"

Katherine Tulpa, *CEO, Association for Coaching*

CREATING THE REFLECTIVE HABIT

Reflection is a critical skill which can enhance the quality of our professional and domestic lives. Yet in a world of "busy," reflective practice often falls to the bottom of the list. We are not alone in the struggle to use the pause button well. This book is here to help.

The book offers a practical toolkit which shows you how to create a sustainable reflective habit. We begin by exploring the meaning and territory of reflection, drawing from the literature to provide context and understanding. The following chapters contain prompts and exercises which will appeal to different processing preferences. The intention throughout this book is firstly, to show that *reflection* means so much more than journaling, and secondly, to encourage an appetite for experimentation that results in a desire to reflect on a regular and sustainable basis. We invite you into an immersive experience, playing with the multitude of reflective possibilities on offer. It is only through repeated trial and error, enlightenment and frustration that we will come to create our own reflective habit.

Written by a coach and coach supervisor, this practical book is an invaluable resource for helping practitioners, but will also be immensely helpful to anyone and everyone who wants to get their pause button in good working order. The book also provides Learning and Development professionals with a suite of tools and materials to help build the reflective practice skill set in their organisation.

Michelle Lucas owns Greenfields Consulting Limited which specialises in executive coaching and the supervision of coaches and supervisors. This is the fourth title she has authored for Routledge.

CREATING THE REFLECTIVE HABIT

A PRACTICAL GUIDE FOR COACHES, MENTORS AND LEADERS

Michelle Lucas

Routledge
Taylor & Francis Group

LONDON AND NEW YORK

Designed cover image: © Charlotte Housden

First published 2023
by Routledge
4 Park Square, Milton Park, Abingdon, Oxon OX14 4RN

and by Routledge
605 Third Avenue, New York, NY 10158

Routledge is an imprint of the Taylor & Francis Group, an informa business

British Library Cataloguing-in-Publication Data
A catalogue record for this book is available from the British Library

Library of Congress Cataloging-in-Publication Data
Names: Lucas, Michael, 1951- author.
Title: Creating the reflective habit : a practical guide for coaches, mentors and leaders / Michelle Lucas.
Description: New York : Routledge, 2023. | Includes bibliographical references and index. |
Identifiers: LCCN 2022056709 (print) | LCCN 2022056710 (ebook) |
ISBN 9781032317595 (hardback) | ISBN 9781032317618 (paperback) |
ISBN 9781003311188 (ebook)
Subjects: LCSH: Critical thinking. | Personal coaching. | Counseling.
Classification: LCC BF441 .L75 2023 (print) | LCC BF441 (ebook) | DDC 153.4/2--dc23/eng/20230209
LC record available at https://lccn.loc.gov/2022056709
LC ebook record available at https://lccn.loc.gov/2022056710

ISBN: 978-1-032-31759-5 (hbk)
ISBN: 978-1-032-31761-8 (pbk)
ISBN: 978-1-003-31118-8 (ebk)

DOI: 10.4324/9781003311188

Typeset in Bembo
by MPS Limited, Dehradun

Leisure by W.H. Davies

What is this life if, full of care,
We have no time to stand and stare.

No time to stand beneath the boughs
And stare as long as sheep or cows.

No time to see, when woods we pass,
Where squirrels hide their nuts in grass.

No time to see, in broad daylight,
Streams full of stars, like skies at night.

No time to turn at Beauty's glance,
And watch her feet, how they can dance.

No time to wait till her mouth can
Enrich that smile her eyes began.

A poor life this is if, full of care,
We have no time to stand and stare.

Source: Davies, W. H. (1911)
Songs of joy and others (No. 7). AC Fifield.

CONTENTS

FIGURES

ABOUT THE AUTHOR

Michelle Lucas is the Director of Greenfields Consulting Limited, specialising in executive coaching, the supervision of coaches and of supervisors and most recently the development of the Regular Reflective Space concept. She has a degree in Applied Psychology from UWIST and an MBA from Warwick Business School. Her early career was in Clinical Psychology before a 20-year career in fast-paced commercial organisations, leading HR functions. Working independently since 2006, she is an Accredited Master Executive Coach and an Accredited Master Coach Supervisor with the Association for Coaching. She completed her training in both coaching (2009) and coaching supervision (2012) at Oxford Brookes University and is now an associate lecturer and coach supervisor for their MA programme. She is a member of the Association of Coaching Supervisors and an active volunteer – in 2020 she conceptualised, then launched and now co-facilitates their innovative Co-Supervision Space. She also volunteers for the Association for Coaching.

Michelle is an innovative practitioner interested in exploring atypical applications of supervision. She is passionate about supporting practitioners to stretch their reflective practice, so that in turn they optimise peer and professional supervision. She is a confident and energetic speaker and has presented annually at the Oxford Brookes International Supervision Conference since 2012. She has written 15 peer-reviewed articles, and is currently deepening her original 2017 research "from Coach to Coach Supervisor mindset". This is the fourth title she has written for Routledge, the previous book was her first editorial role and the first two books were collaborations with David Clutterbuck, Carol Whitaker and Tammy Turner.

She lives in Weymouth, Dorset, UK, with her husband Mark, and two dogs Tia (a chocolate Labrador) and Colin (a rescued Daschund).

CONTRIBUTORS

Linda Aspey is an executive coach, facilitator, supervisor, therapist, writer and leadership development specialist with a long career in supporting personal, team and organisational change. She has a Masters in HR, is global faculty at Time to Think (teaching the Thinking Environment®), a fellow and registered member of BACP (FBACP/MBACP), and a Work that Reconnects ("Active Hope") facilitator. Since 2018 Linda has specialised in climate change and the environment, working across the fields of climate psychology, mental health, awareness and action.

Jo Bond is a highly experienced leadership coach and supervisor. She has coached more than 600 individuals from over 120 organisations, including leading global and UK corporates, start-up ventures, and public sector bodies. Her clients span 30 nationalities and seniority levels up to board directors. Jo's business experience began in aviation, then senior, international leadership roles in financial and consulting firms. Jo's academic studies started with a Biology BSc, followed by Master's degrees from LSE and INSEAD in HR and Coaching, respectively. She is an EMCC Master Practitioner Coach, HULT-qualified coaching and consulting supervisor, and a CIPD Chartered Fellow.

Judy Brown is a leadership development expert best known for her work in dialogue and reflective practice. Her two leadership books are *A Leader's Guide to Reflective Practice* and the *Art and Spirit of Leadership*. She has also published several books of her poetry. She lives in the United States on a tidal creek off the Chesapeake Bay where she enjoys kayaking. She can be contacted via her website: www.judysorumbrown.com.

Hannah Butler, MSc, PGCE, BA(Hon), is a professional accredited coaching and the current director of knowledge exchange with the EMCC UK. Her professional background spans over 20 years of educational leadership and she now runs her own coaching company, providing leadership coaching and coach training. She has worked as a coach across all sectors, has an MSc in Coaching and Mentoring and is a certified master practitioner for strengths scoping. She plays a key role in the development of coaching, mentoring and supervision in the United Kingdom through the delivery of ILM Qualification, short course and her national work for the EMCC UK. Hannah has recently completed research into Independent Reflective Practice and how this impacts coaching practice. She has a strong belief that Independent Reflective Practice is an art form that develops over time, enriching and developing our understanding of coaching and enhancing the experience for our clients. Being present, wrestling with the difficult and clearing the path in her reflective practice has continually impacted the way she works. She is constantly bowled over by the power of reflection, our ability to hold of space for ourselves and our willingness to engage in the hard work and dedication to transform the way we work.

Henry Campion is an independent coaching co-visor. He is a qualified doctor, counsellor, executive coach and coach supervisor. In his work with coaches and other supervisors, he seeks to deepen awareness of self and others, and of how to use the power of relationship in nurturing learning and growth. See www.co-visor.com.

Christine Champion founded acumen executive coaching in 2003, based in the City of London, and is a coaching supervisor in the Masters program in Coaching and Mentoring at Oxford Brookes University. A passionate and experienced, executive coach; her organisation is focused on the postmodern approaches drawn from Vertical Development approaches and how these can be applied in the development of leaders and coaches to be fit for the future in an increasingly, dynamic, uncertain and ambiguous world. The starting point for coaching is designed to increase self-knowledge, insight and awareness which in turn elevates levels of consciousness, enabling the individual to intentionally choose how to respond in different situations. This enhancement of consciousness moves the individual away from old habitual and learned responses to create and embed greater resourcefulness, agility and flexibility which is required for successful leadership in today's environments.

David Crowe is the director of Crowe Associates which he started in 2000. Over the past 22 years, David has developed and specialised in 1-1 and coaching supervision. David works 1-1 with a range of people in the public and private sectors, coaching them in business improvement, career change, personal development and building confidence.

Claire Davey has worked in the United Kingdom and internationally as an executive coach, supervisor and development consultant for global organisations within professional services, the financial sector, education, telecommunications, the third sector and elite sport. Prior to starting CDPerformance Ltd., she was head of Coaching & Executive Development at Deloitte where she pioneered systemic team coaching, experimented with external and internal supervision and was an early adopter of supervision on supervision. Claire served as a governor and NED of the EMCC UK where she both encouraged and enabled advances in the world of coaching and supervision. She completed her supervision studies with The Bath Consultancy Group, specialising in Transcultural Supervision and Supervising Teams and Organisations. She has an integrative approach to supervision that encourages enquiry and experimentation often through a creative approach and with ecology in mind.

Sue Dawson is an experienced movement teacher and coach, specialising in somatics and embodiment. Her teaching integrates her life-long commitment to movement with her belief in approaching each teaching session as an opportunity to explore the connections between body, mind and soul. Both her teaching and her coaching aim to help her clients uncover hidden barriers and fixed thought patterns, in turn bringing greater focus and resilience and finding greater peace. Sue has been teaching Yoga and Pilates for over 30 years in London, Bristol, Somerset and

Devon. She runs wellbeing retreats and runs weekly online and in person coaching, yoga and pilates sessions. She was a teacher at the Bristol Old Vic Theatre School for 17 years and has worked for other acting schools, professional rugby and osteopath wellbeing centres and is a contributor on a worldwide meditation app. www.sensegreaterpeace.co.uk

Liz Ford is an accredited master executive coach and an accredited coaching supervisor. She loves using creative methods in her work and often uses the outdoors with her clients. She has shared her interest in using these techniques by contributing to a number of coaching/supervision-related books and publications. When she's not working Liz enjoys walking in the hills, reading crime novels and listening to music. She also sings with a local choir and loves going to the theatre.

Nicholas Gordon is a poet and the webmaster of the popular poetry website, Poems for Free. He holds an MA and a PhD in English and American Literature from Stanford University and a BA in English from Queens College of the City University of New York. For many years until his retirement, he taught literature and writing at New Jersey City University in Jersey City, New Jersey. His poetry, fiction, biography, and drama may all be read for free at his website, and much of it is available as videos on his YouTube channel, also Poems for Free, and for purchase in paperback from Amazon. You can follow him on Facebook at PoemsbyNicholasGordon and join his email list at https://medium.com/subscribe/@nickgo_89269.

Pauline Greystone has over 25 years of experience as an entrepreneur, coach and facilitator. She founded her own company 20 years ago and has built it into a highly successful enterprise – based in Brussels providing leadership and coaching programmes for major EU and other international public sector organisations. She has an MBA and an MSc in Coaching and Behavioural Change and has managed to combine her extensive experience in managing a fast-growing business while developing her own coaching and training expertise – focusing on areas such as resilience, new leadership challenges and women's potential.

Anita Hayne, FCIPD, is an independent accredited professional executive coach and coach supervisor. Her coaching career started as an L&D professional in a multinational technology organisation and developed in senior HR roles including being a designated coach on an international management programme. As an independent coach, consultant & coach supervisor for over the last 20 years she has coached on management programmes, delivered group supervision, completed numerous individual coaching and supervision assignments, including specialist coaching in the wellbeing and neuro-diversity field.

Abigail Heathcote is a bilingual (English/French) coach and trainer based in Paris, working in international and multicultural environments to support managers and their teams to achieve greater levels of trust, alignment and collaboration, even when working remotely. Trained in Clean Language by Judy Rees, Caitlin Walker and Marian Way, Abigail is passionate about Clean Language and its potential in organisations. She has used it successfully in the public and private sectors to support teams and groups to develop a culture of listening and attention to difference, helping them to increase mutual understanding, even in conflict, and to make better, more inclusive decisions.

Jackee Holder, a London-born and raised, enjoys the diversity and richness of urban living. Her multi-layered portfolio includes her work as an executive corporate coach, writer and published author of five non-fiction titles and anthologies. Jackee facilitates leadership and wellbeing courses and workshops. A nature and tree lover, she brings the world of nature into her coaching and therapeutic work. She is the curator and host of the online Paper Therapy course and the Tuesday early morning women's weekly writing circle. Jackee writes a monthly journaling column, *The Write To Flourish for Psychologies Magazine* (UK). Twitter: @jackeeholder; Instagram: @jackeeholderinspires

Charlotte Housden, MSc, CPsychol, AFBPsS, is an occupational and coaching psychologist, supporting executives and individuals at crossroads in their careers and lives. She also works with organisations to build and implement global executive coaching and senior leadership development programmes. Over two years,

Charlotte interviewed 100+ people from 27 countries who were going through transitions in their lives, then wrote a book about their stories and successes, called *Swim, Jump, Fly: A Guide to Changing Your Life.*

Alastair Kidd is an experienced leadership and team coach, and systemic group facilitator, with a previous commercial background in technology and IT services. All his work is centred on promoting a more conscious practice of leadership – he describes the essence of this as *having one real conversation after another, witnessing people, and supporting them to witness themselves.* He works with leaders and teams from global mega-corps to small enterprises, from purpose-driven sole practitioners to not-for-profits and social enterprises. You can find out more about Alastair along with other poetry and thinking on his website: www.alastairkidd.com.

Claire Kitay, MA (Oxon), PGDip RNCM, PGDip Music Therapy GSMD, is a professional freelance musician and HCPC registered music therapist. Having studied and trained in the UK and Switzerland, she has examined for the ABRSM and worked in the NHS and education as a therapist for over 25 years. She has a music therapy supervision practice, performs as a solo organ recitalist and contributes regularly to a professional music journal. Her experience in a wide range of music therapy settings led to running workshops in professional development and group dynamics.

Margaret Macafee, CPsychol AFBPsS CPBP, is an occupational psychologist, accredited executive coach and organisational development specialist. Her varied consulting portfolio includes a range of UK-based, multi-national and global clients. She served on the Committee of the British Psychological Society's Division in Coaching Psychology between 2012 and 2017, coordinating Peer Practice Groups (PPG) for coaches around the UK. She has co-hosted a thriving London-based PPG community for the past 12 years. In partnership with Hogrefe, she created a set of cards to support the interpretation of the NEO Personality Inventory (NEO-PI-3). For her latest creative collaboration, she has found the natural world to be rich in generative possibilities for coaches and supervisors.

Elaine Patterson is a master coach, supervisor and writer at The Centre for Reflection and Creativity Ltd. Elaine takes her inspiration from her love of the arts, history, mediation, writing, poetry, Kayaking, Wild Swimming and Nordic walking. Elaine's book *"Reflect to Create! - The Dance of Reflection for Creative Leadership, Professional Practice and Supervision"* (and its accompanying Workbooks) encapsulates her kind vision which is to bring the creative powers of reflection to everyone everywhere for inspiration, healing and wisdom.

Ted Perry is the Fletcher professor of the Arts Emeritus at Middlebury College, Middlebury, Vermont, USA. Before Middlebury, he was the director of the Film Department at the Museum of Modern Art in New York City and also chair of the Cinema Studies Department at New York University.

Stéphane Pigeon was born in Brussels, Belgium, in December 1970 and received the degree of electrical engineering from the Université Catholique de Louvain in June 1994, with a specialisation in signal processing. He finalised a PhD thesis in the field of multimodal biometric person authentication in 1999. Then, Stéphane joined the Royal Military Academy as a part-time researcher, working on various topics such as computer-assisted person identification, data fusion, channel coding, audio processing, speech segmentation and language identification. In parallel, he worked as an exclusive consultant for Roland Corporation Japan, in the area of electronic musical instruments. His spare time has always been devoted to trying out new ideas. He started myNoise.net in 2014, a free source of non-distracting noises and music on the Internet. One year later, when myNoise.net became a big success, attracting thousands of users every day, Stéphane decided to work full-time for the project, and he still does today.

Marie Quigley is the co-founder of Empower World, an international coach training and leadership organization based in the United Kingdom, with hubs in the Middle East and Australia. She is an ICF master certified coach and accredited coach supervisor (ESIA) with over 27 years of international experience. She provides executive coaching, leadership training as well as professional coach training, mentoring and supervision to coaches around the globe.

As a former graphic designer and art director – creativity and experimentation are at the heart and soul of her work.

Helen Robson is an experienced and qualified coach and coach supervisor. A former book editor, Helen then worked in L&D functions in large organisations before setting up her own consultancy, Brightlight Coaching & Consulting. Helen gained a distinction in her Post Graduate Certificate in Business and Executive Coaching, particularly gravitating to the Gestalt/Psychodynamic approaches to the work. Her career in executive coaching, supervision and leadership development continues to inspire her and deepen her beliefs in how coaching can enable, enrich and support people and organisations. In addition, her commitment to the industry has led her to take up an associate lecturer post. Having lived and worked in the UK and South Africa, Helen has now settled in Somerset.

Paul Sanbar is an ingenuity + executive coach, coaching supervisor, and hands-on visual thinking facilitator, Paul Sanbar's life and career have been dedicated to the field of self-development and to effecting positive change through purposeful play and powerful conversations initially as a humanistic psychotherapist and for the last ten years as a credentialed coach and certified coaching supervisor. A certified LEGO® Serious Play® methods facilitator/coach and a member of the MURAL Consultant Network, he believes that sustainable systemic development occurs when individuals and teams think and reflect not only with words but also with their eyes and hands, putting their imagination to work in both tactile and technological ways.

Louise Schubert has spent the last 40 years working as a specialist in Learning and Development, initially within the hospitality industry, where her roots lie. She gained her MSc in Organisation Consulting at Ashridge and is accredited with the EMCC as a coach at the senior practitioner level and has her ESIA as a coach supervisor. Her current practice is a blend of leadership development workshops, executive coaching, and supervision in local projects where her home is, in Spain, or globally in a virtual environment. She resources her work with activities based on nature and from her Resilience Coaching toolkit.

David Tinker, MSc, Dip Supr, has 20 years of experience in leadership development, coaching, and supervision. His own training includes mask, shadow work, sociodrama, storytelling and Clean Language. He trained as a supervisor with the London School of Psychodrama and designed the Rethinkly software which is used for corporate coaching and in support of mental health treatment in the NHS. David's background in visual and embodied story-telling has been translated into immersive learning concepts in the Metaverse.

Carol Whitaker is an AC accredited supervisor and has over 15 years supervising both 1-1 & Groups including Oxford Brookes University Students doing their MA in Coaching and Mentoring Practice, ILM7 Executive Coaching PG Cert and their internal coaching programmes. Her portfolio covers Coaching, Team/Group Coaching and Coach Supervision, Mentoring and facilitation. Her early career was in Human Resources, she has experience at the Board level, various NED roles, and an MBA. She has co-authored two 5*rated books *"Coaching Supervision: A Practical Guide for Supervisees"* (2016) and *"Peer Supervision in Coaching & Mentoring: A Versatile Guide for Reflective Practice"* (2018). Both were published by Routledge and the Peer Supervision Chapter in *Coaching & Mentoring Supervision: Theory and Practice,* 2nd Edition (2021). Her website is www.whitaker-consulting.co.uk.

PREFACE

Reflection fuels a humility that encourages me to acknowledge multiple perspectives and the inevitability of things unseen. For me, the process enables me to see more than I saw at the time. Perhaps like me, you have attempted to galvanise yourself, to be more disciplined, to promise to create firmer boundaries and separate out the time to reflect. Yet in a world of "busy," reflective practice often falls to the bottom of the list. We are not alone in the struggle to use the pause button well. This book is here to help.

My intention through this book is two-fold. First to dispel the myth that reflection is synonymous with journalling. Second to encourage an appetite for experimentation that results in a desire to reflect on a regular and sustainable basis.

These intentions emanate from my journey as a reflective practitioner. Despite being more introverted, I have struggled to create an independent reflective practice for myself. The implicit assumption through my coach and coach supervision training was that reflection was achieved through journaling. While I almost always uncovered something new, this was not enough to create a ritual for reflection. As a supervisor, I felt hypocritical encouraging others to journal while knowing my own reluctance to do the same. I tried diarising protected time, yet when the time came, something else grabbed my attention. By contrast, I noticed that if I had peer or professional supervision, I prepared, it happened and I enjoyed it! Expressing my thoughts in the presence of another, the conversation liberated insights.

Meeting Charlotte Housden in 2018 who is both a psychologist and a photographer was an important influence in my reflective practice. We explored how imagery helped take client conversations to a deeper place, acting as a muse for exploring what lies just beyond our conscious thought. With the help of Charlotte's images, I became motivated to engage in individual reflection. It seemed uncanny that once drawn to an image and exploring it for a while, new information often emerged. Eventually, I realised that I wasn't "bad" at reflection, rather that written reflection was not my preferred processing style. This freed me up to experiment with different kinds of visual cues to build my reflective practice. By extension, I also encouraged my supervisees to consider how their own processing preferences might inform their individual reflective practice.

Then in 2019, I was editing the book, 101 Coaching Supervision Techniques, Approaches, Enquiries and Experiments. I signposted each technique as to whether it applied to individual supervision or group supervision, peer or professional supervision. In so doing, I recognised that some techniques could be used independently i.e. self-supervision. Marketing this book in 2020, I looked for opportunities to bring the techniques to life. Through the Association for Coaching Supervisors, I developed the concept of Co-Supervision and ran monthly sessions which showcased a selection of individual supervision techniques. Through my own business, Greenfields Consulting Limited, I developed the concept of Group Supervision Experimentation Labs. Quarterly sessions that showcased the group supervision techniques.

Later in 2020, I embarked on an experiment. Recognising my own difficulty in setting aside regular protected time for reflection, I wanted to offer a service which provided that for others. I also wanted to encourage practitioners to experiment with approaches that included, but went beyond, written reflections. A pilot workshop went well, and the Regular Reflective Practice Space sessions were born. Initially I relied on the self-supervision techniques from the 101 book, alongside a few templates from my own library. It was also an opportunity to share Charlotte's imagery and conscious that not everyone likes working in silence, I included some background music options. As the months went on, I broadened the range of reflective prompts to include poetry and kinaesthetic approaches.

The feedback from these sessions was heartening, participants loved the freshness that this approach brought to their reflections. Participants were generous, sharing materials from their own libraries. About six months later, I noticed that it was possible to offer a suite of new resources each month that deliberately emphasised the range of processing styles. The library of resources continues to grow. So, in the spirit of sharing these resources with an increasingly larger community, the proposal for this book was formed.

ACKNOWLEDGEMENTS

This book would not have come into being without the encouragement and support of numerous colleagues and clients and participants of the Reflective Practice Space sessions. It has been a joy to experiment and collaborate with everyone involved.

Those people who have directly contributed to the content have been acknowledged in the list of contributors. So, here I would like to mention some of the unsung heroes.

Firstly, thanks to my steadfast VA, Emma Conway-Hyde. Emma not only attended to the detail that regularly passed me by, but she also became quite the detective, to ensure we secured the formal permission from poets and other original author's work.

Next, I have to thank an army of peer reviewers. Helen Robson, for keeping my head up and out of the weeds, thinking through how the whole book hung together. David Tinker for bringing his language skills so diligently to my rubbish grammar as well as opening my eyes to additional references. Finally, the members of the book club from the Association of Coaching Supervisors (Michael Cullen, Pamela Fay and Kate Pinder) who gave feedback on drafts, that were far from perfect, so generously.

Over the beautiful summer, a round of golf was the perfect antidote to a cluttered head and my tired "been-at-the-screen-too-long" eyes. So, I must also mention my golfing buddies Sam and Pauline from the Came Down Academy here in Dorset. The fresh air and the hilarity and humility of being novice golfers, enabled me to return to my desk recharged and ready to tackle the manuscript again.

Finally, a huge thanks to my husband Mark for his unwavering support and his graceful acceptance that taking the laptop to Spain (on holiday!) really was the best way to manage my anxiety about finalising the book in good time.

Thank you all.

INTRODUCTION – HOW TO USE THIS BOOK

The word "reflection" is such a commonly used term, that it would be easy to assume we all know what it means. However, the artform that is reflective practice encompasses multiple ideas and concepts. Before we dive into the application of reflective prompts, Chapter 1 takes a contextual view on what reflective practice is. Drawing from existing literature and research to provide a common understanding and to frame what follows.

What follows is organised into sections according to the processing style of the reflective prompts provided.

Cognitive: These prompts encourage you to use the written word. Each one builds on the traditional and emergent form of journalling by offering a structure that can ignite and layer your ideas.

Visual: These prompts invite you to observe a variety of visual stimuli, exploiting the notion that images implicitly convey more information than other forms of communication.

Auditory: These encourage you to open your ears to both familiar and unfamiliar sounds. Increasingly, the coaching community is taking inspiration from the natural world. Many of the soundscapes build on this idea.

Kinaesthetic: These prompts seek to engage with your body more than your thoughts. The senses of physical touch and movement are emphasised here. They take a more holistic approach and aim to place attention on your somatic self, to access further wisdom.

DOI: 10.4324/9781003311188-1

Poetic: There are many poetic forms, rhythm and rhyme, ballads, blank verse and even limericks. Indeed Flanagan (2019) observed that "perhaps the characteristic most central to the definition of poetry is its unwillingness to be defined, labelled, or nailed down." He continues ... "Poetry is the chiselled marble of language. It is a paint-spattered canvas, but the poet uses words instead of paint, *and the canvas is you.*" Indeed, it was the potential of poetry to trigger a subjective response which felt useful as a reflective prompt.

Each of us will come to this book with our existing preferences and assumptions about what is likely to be effective for us. So, before providing the prompts, I offer some gentle encouragement, positioning the potential merits of each processing style. The format for the content differs slightly across the sections. However, typically each will start with a box suggesting example topics for reflection. Then, I share a little of how the prompt came to my attention, sometimes sharing the insights it provoked for me. Each prompt provides "A pathway for reflection" i.e. guidance on how you could choose to use the material. This is not a method to adhere to, rather a suggestion on how you might form your own experiment. Use it, ignore it, adapt it ... it is up to you. The reflective material is included either within the text or signposted in the resources section. Additional resources are identified where appropriate and finally References and Further Reading are noted. At the end of each of the five reflective prompt sections, I share some anecdotes from participants of our Regular Reflective Practice Space sessions. I hope this brings to life how a moment of reflection can serve to significantly shape a practitioner's client work.

There are 12 reflective prompts in each section – providing you with the ingredients for a year of experimentation. My invitation is to create a space each month where you can reflect on your practice. Ideally, gift yourself an hour, if that seems impossible, start with whatever time you have.

I am grateful to the many colleagues who have contributed content. I acknowledge those who brought the material to my attention, I reference other practitioner's material in the appropriate way and where the reflective prompt has been developed by someone else, that is clarified at the start.

Some readers may already have an approach to their reflective practice which suits them well. For those who have not, Chapter 2, supports you to self-coach, to engage with your experimental experiences so that you emerge clearer in how you can create a sustainable reflective habit.

My hope is that the book will appeal to many different types of helping practitioners and supervisors. It might also be useful to organisational L&D teams who are seeking resources for their employees, or to leaders who are open to exploring the complexity of their roles and relationships.

Written by a coach and coach supervisor there is undoubtedly a "helping practitioner" flavour to this book, yet our reader is anyone and everyone who wants to understand how to get their pause button in good working order. Reflection is a critical skill which can enhance the quality of our professional and domestic lives. This book helps you discover how you can create a reflective habit that will genuinely bring value for you.

REFERENCE

Flanagan, M. (2019) *What is Poetry, and How Is It Different?* Available at: https://www.thoughtco.com/what-is-poetry-852737. (Accessed: 11 August 2022).

UNDERSTANDING THE TERRITORY OF REFLECTIVE PRACTICE

By Hannah Butler

Before embarking on your experimental journey towards creating a sustainable reflective habit, this chapter reviews the literature and

- Outlines what reflective practice is
- Considers why reflective practice is helpful for practitioners and leaders alike
- Observes how the nature of reflection changes over time
- Offers a range of focal points for reflection
- Challenges the current bias in the coaching community towards written journalling and makes the case for expanding reflective practice with more creative activities
- Explores two models which may help articulate how reflection matures over time

WHAT IS REFLECTIVE PRACTICE?

Bassot (2016, p. 2) contends that our daily meanderings do not constitute reflective practice. While her point is arguable, the type of reflection referred to in this book, has a greater sense of deliberateness.

> Reflective practice is an iterative, open-ended, creative process, where we take deliberate conscious time to explore and interrogate our practice in a systematic and systemic way. This enables us to adapt what we do and consider how we might develop our future practice, in service of our stakeholders.

DOI: 10.4324/9781003311188-2

This stance has been influenced by the work of Schön (1983, p. 43) who presents reflection as a messy, rather than a precise activity, as he puts it:

> There are those who choose the swampy lowlands. They deliberately involve themselves in messy but crucially important problems and, when asked to describe their methods of inquiry, they speak of experience, trial and error, intuition, and muddling through.

Schön (1983) invites us to engage in a position of disequilibrium, avoiding judgement and searching for new evidence on which to reconstruct our practice. He states that this requires patience, dedicated time, balancing discipline and freedom.

The work of the educator Ghaye (2010, pp. 1–3) is helpful and equally applicable to coaches, mentors and leaders. He presents six key features of reflective practice and comments that it

1   Makes links between practice and the development of practice
2   Connects the cognitive, emotional and active elements
3   Supports structured or organised thinking
4   Takes place within various time zones (past, present, future)
5   Illuminates our strengths
6   Is a way of identifying and working with our triggers

While reflection may appear to be an individual process, Thompson and Thompson (2018, pp. 4–9) state that it need not be a solitary pursuit and can be enhanced through working with others. Similarly, Turner et al. (2018, p. 36) comment that "reflecting with others can accelerate reflection by identifying blindspots, patterns of behaviour and strengths that can be enhanced." Observing coaches (and other helping professionals) they engage in numerous types of reflective activities which include the following:

• Supervision – both peer and professional
• Reflective pairs
• Reflective practice groups or communities of practice
• Independent reflective practice (the focus of this book)

Pause

What are the elements of your own reflective practice?

Which ones do you derive most value from? And how?

WHY IS REFLECTIVE PRACTICE IMPORTANT?

The phrase VUCA (Volatile, Uncertain, Complex and Ambiguous, see Hicks and Townsend, 2002) has been used to describe our current context. Our pace of life seems to continually quicken and the focus for many executive coaches is supporting leaders who are experiencing overwhelm. In response, practitioners are bringing mindfulness, resilience and wellbeing practices into their coaching toolkit. Regardless of this context, we know that coaching assignments are complex. Even experienced coaches must make choices about which avenues of conversation to pursue, which inevitably means that many more avenues are left unexplored.

All of the professional coaching bodies include reflective practice as a critical component of the coaching skill set. In looking at the literature, the benefits of doing so are captured by Thompson and Thompson (2018, p. 25) who identify three possible outcomes from reflection:

- Immanent reflection – reflective practice that does not create change in our practice, this is not to say it is pointless, just that there is no change
- Transitive reflection – reflective practice that induces a change in our practice, this could be related to the tools and techniques we employ in our coaching
- Transformational reflection – reflective practice that changes practice and can transform the way we work, therefore eliminating a problem or embedding new practices

However, it can be difficult to know what the outcome of any given reflection might be, until we have completed it. Indeed it may take multiple reflective moments before reflection culminates in insight or change.

Taking a broader view, we can position reflective practice, as a form of supervision. With this lens, we can then consider its purpose in three broad segments. What follows observes Proctor's (1986) nomenclature of Formative i.e. a vehicle for our development; Normative i.e. a means of ensuring ethical practice; and Restorative i.e. a space for re-balancing our energies.

A formative perspective

This is about our "well-knowing." Bassot (2016, pp. 2–4) describes how reflective practice enables us to "strive for excellence." She suggests that it enables us to flex and integrate new ideas, avoid inertia and keep our practice in a state of constant growth. Exploring and integrating research to inform our work is important. However, research seldom offers direct instructions on integration into practice. Thompson and Thompson (2018) suggest that reflection is useful to enable us to play with concepts and theory to establish our own framework for practice.

A normative perspective

This is about our "well-doing." A key feature of coaching work is that it is largely carried out in isolation – just the coach and the client(s) engaging in dialogue. Reflection provides an opportunity to create distance from our own perspective. According to George (2021), this distance allows us to present ourselves with some difficult questions which can raise our awareness of the ethical positions we can take and how this can play out in terms of power. Similarly, Hawkins and Shohet's (2012) Seven-Eyed Model is particularly useful as a reflection tool, to explore situations from alternative points of view. Each eye can be addressed systematically in order to broaden our understanding and help us avoid contamination of the space with colluded and fixed thinking.

It is naive to think that we can eliminate our biases and assumptions through solitary reflection. However, reflection does allow us to recognise when old habits and assumptions are continuing to tap us on the shoulder. A signal that we can no longer, independently, reach the itch that needs to be scratched, and a reminder to engage with others to calibrate and enhance our continued reflection.

A restorative perspective

This is about our "wellbeing." There is limited comment on the restorative benefits of reflective practice. In a systematic review by Bachkirova et al. (2020) of the coaching supervision literature only one of 68 sources, was concerned with this. The authors, Graßmann and Schermuly (2018), offered tentative findings that supervision could, in part, mitigate the impact of emotional labour for novice coaches. Similar, yet tentative evidence, comes from Dehlin and Lundh (2018) who found that while reflection was important for compassion satisfaction it did not appear to protect against compassion fatigue, burnout or secondary traumatic stress.

As tempting as it may be to join in the world of "busy," the hallmark of a professional coach or helping practitioner is to find space to pause. This equally applies to leaders. In that space, we are able to slow down, review past and anticipate future choices. This brings more into our awareness such that we operate in "conscious competence" (Broadwell, 1969) for more of the time.

Pause

What benefits have you experienced from reflection?

Why might slowing down to review your work be useful to you? Your clients? Your organisation?

WHEN DO WE REFLECT?

While the working assumption is often that reflection will happen after a client session, several authors identify that professional reflection is more than looking back on events. Figure 1.1 brings those perspectives together illustrating how the direction of our reflection changes over time.

Figure 1.1 starts with Thompson and Thompon's (2018) concept of "reflection for action" which is future focused. This is the planning and thinking about what we might do in our next session with a client. Next, Schön (1983) presents us with the

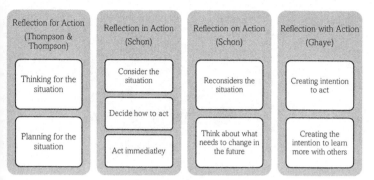

Figure 1.1 Reflection through time

principles of "in action" and "on action." The former requires that reflection is contemporaneous. This reflection is done in the moment and requires "tacit knowledge" i.e. the type of knowledge that can only be gained in and through practice. Here practitioners hold the process and recognise the need to flex and move within a session, to be of service to the client. Reflection on action is the third and more common interpretation of reflective practice, the idea that we reflect on events after they have occurred.

Finally, Ghaye (2010) offers a fourth step, "reflection-with-action," which in itself contains two meanings. The first is about creating intention, for example making the decision to practice using a new approach and taking action, deciding when, how and with which client. The second meaning invites us to consider when the utility of independent reflection has been exhausted and we make the decision to seek additional support through peer reflection or supervision. Ghaye (2010, p. 7) notes that "There are limits to learning and acting alone. Often the power to change and improve something is better achieved by a group or team."

When we consider the dimension of time, it highlights how reflecting on any single moment in our work, is unlikely to be an isolated event. The Spiralling the Field model of Turner and Lucas (2023) illustrates how reflection on a moment may have many influences and will become richer through multiple touchpoints over time (see Figure 1.2). Rather than see reflective practice as linear, their use of a spiral invites us to consider how our reflections ebb,

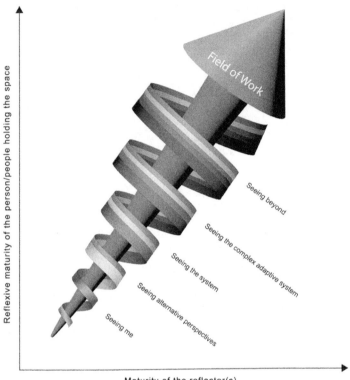

Spiralling the field to develop reflexivity

© Turner and Lucas (2022)

Figure 1.2 Spiralling the field

flow and circle back, building an increasingly robust (but rarely exhaustive) perspective over time.

Pause

What proportion of your reflections happen … Before? During? After? With action?

How would you characterise the nature of your reflection at each of these time positions?

WHAT DO WE FOCUS OUR ATTENTION ON?

Once we have created the space in which to reflect, we then consider what to place our reflective attention upon. This is a complex choice. The prompts in the chapters ahead are intended to facilitate this process. Some direct your attention quite specifically, others invite you to create an environment in which reflections are more likely to emerge. Most of them require you to bring some form of material with which to start.

In reviewing the literature, a number of topics are identified which offer a focus for our reflective attention. From the education field four topics are highlighted, which are largely introspective (i.e. the examination of one's own thoughts, feelings and sensations), they are expanded upon next. Additionally, authors from the coaching community offer five topics which are largely extrospective (i.e. the examination or observation of what is outside oneself) and are also articulated next.

LOOKING INWARDS

Emotions

Gibbs (1998) pioneered the inclusion of the affective process into his experiential learning cycle (see pages 54–56). Gibbs contends that reflective practice takes more than thinking and doing alone. His model offers six distinctly different questions, the second asks "What were you thinking and feeling?" This explicit inclusion of emotion suggests that we need an understanding that our emotions may play a part in our capacity or incapacity to reflect and change. The work of Moon (2004) reminds us to treat our feelings with the same respect and examination as our thinking, commenting that emotions can impede our ability to be objectively engaged in the learning process.

Strengths

A common assumption in reflective practice is that we are looking for errors or flaws that we can correct. Ghaye (2010) offers us an alternative view, coming from the perspective of positive psychology he differentiates between deficit and strength-based approaches. In his 4-stage model (see pages 58–59) he poses questions which mirror the Appreciative Inquiry of Cooperrider and Whitney (2000). Rather than engage in self-criticism, it encourages us to leverage our existing competence and confidence. From this more positive base, we may then become more open, Ghaye (2010) notes that this enables us to release our grip on previously held thoughts and feelings such that development can emerge.

Knowledge and justification

The Reflective Judgement Model of King and Kitchener (1994) identifies three main developmental stages (which are then subdivided). Each stage draws attention to two key elements – knowledge and justification.

The 1st stage, Pre-Reflective Thinking is where knowledge is seen as concrete and certain, any uncertainty can be resolved through gaining knowledge from an authority figure. Practitioners at this stage see justification as superflous because any knowledge held is seen as true. At the 2nd Quasi-reflective Stage, the practitioner begins to see that knowledge is uncertain because any evidence will be influenced by individual, situational and contextual factors. Justifcation for their position will also be idiosyncratic and any conclusions drawn may lack coherence as all evidence will be held as important. The 3rd stage, Reflective Thinking, is where knowledge will be constructed by the individual based on reasonable evaluation. Justification is developed through comparing and contrasting information and through deciding what is most plausible taking multiple factors into account. In Figure 1.3, the model is applied to a coaching example.

The King and Kitchener model was developed in the context of adolescent and adult development. Nonetheless, understanding these stages may help practitioners recognise the characteristics of reflection at a moment in time. It is possible to move around the stages to expand what is noticed.

King & Kitchener Stages		Coaching Example "Does good coaching always start with a clear goal?"
Pre-Reflective Thinking	Stage 1	*Yes it does*
	Stage 2	*Yes it does, because my tutor said so.*
	Stage 3	*Yes it does, because my tutor told me that Professor Knowitall conducted research and found it to be true.*
Quasi-Reflective Thinking	Stage 4	*Possibly, because the tutor from my other unit said that Professor Knowitall research was flawed due to the fact that he only studied his own coaching cases*
	Stage 5	*Maybe, Yes in my opinion. However I realise that there maybe views that are equally valid and different to my own.*
Reflective Thinking	Stage 6	*It is difficult to be sure. There is a wealth of research offering alternative points of view. However, given the research and my practice I feel there is place for both.*
	Stage 7	*Yes and No because I have read the research to both positions and also attended training on Goal and Soft Focus Setting. I have tried and tested the approaches in my coaching, discussed this work in supervision and concluded that I use what is in service of the client at any given point in time.*

Figure 1.3 King and Kitchener's reflective judgement model (1994), using a coaching example

Assumptions

Brookfield (2016, p. 2) coined the phrase "assumption hunting" to describe how we peel back the layers of what first appears to be true. For example, we may work with a client and find them hostile and ambivalent to the coaching experience, however, in reflection we notice we are holding an underlying assumption, for example, that they needed no explanation of how coaching works. Taking notice of our assumptions invites us to get more curious about our client and nurtures introspection.

Adding to the depth of our understanding, Mezirow (1998, p. 185) outlined how a critical reflection of our assumptions leads to us thinking for ourselves "rather than acting on the concepts, value and thinking of others." He goes on to identify seven different types of assumption of increasing depth and complexity. Figure 1.4 provides an illustration of how we might apply these different levels of assumptions to a coaching example. This examination enables us to critically reflect on our assumptions, question their validity which may then enable a different path of thinking and ultimately prompt transformational learning.

Category	Description	Example Question for Coaches
Level 1. Reflectivity	• Understanding our point of view • Question how our thoughts might influence our behaviours	• What do I believe about the client/relationship/subject…? • How is this impacting my coaching?
Level 2. Affective Reflectivity	• Understanding our emotions and our emotions about our emotions • Questioning our emotions, triggers and their effective use	• How do I feel in relation to my coaching? • How are these feelings enabling and/or impeding the coaching?
Level 3. Discriminant Reflectivity	• Understanding our perception of others • Questioning whether the perception is valid and reasonable	• To what extent are my perceptions accurate? • How do I know this?
Level 4. Judgemental Reflectivity	• Understanding our core values and how these shape our judgements • Questions the judgements made as a result of this value	• What are my values? • How are these guiding my judgements on this client/relationship/subject?
Level 5. Conceptual Reflectivity	• Understanding our thoughts and beliefs are constructed • Question why these thoughts and beliefs exist	• How do I explain my patterns of thinking and beliefs? • Where did I learn that?
Level 6. Psychic Reflectivity	• Understanding our predjudice and stereotypes • Question how educated our conclusions are	• What are my immediate judgements in relation to the client /relationship/subject …? • What will best inform my conclusions?
Level 7. Theoretical Reflectivity	• Understanding our assumptions are based upon culture, learning experiences • Questions whether it is reasonable to hold these assumptions	• What are my assumptions in relation to the client/relationship/subject? • How are my assumptions serving me, my client, my stakeholder?

Figure 1.4 Mezirow (1998) levels of reflectivity, in a coaching context

LOOKING OUTWARDS

From the coaching community, Turner and Lucas (2022) take a more contextual perspective and invite the reflector to consider both their inner world and material that arises from the context (or field) of practice. In their model (see Figure 1.2), they offer the following five **focal** points for reflection:

1   Seeing me: reflection upon the self
2   Seeing alternative perspectives: extending our perceptions of ourselves and others in the field
3   Seeing the system: using our own and others' perspectives to reflect upon the entire field where the coaching is taking place
4   Seeing the complex adaptive system: considering systems within systems and how they both affect and are affected by each other; reflecting upon the dynamics and interdependencies of the elements within the field(s)
5   Seeing beyond: probing the field with a future focus for the implication of what lies ahead as a result of the systemic understanding and what's unfolding within the complexity as we know it currently

As mentioned at the start of this chapter, reflective practice comes in many forms – we may reflect alone we may reflect with others. As you move through the book it is important not to conflate the type of reflection with the focus of reflection. This book offers 60 reflective prompts designed for use in independent reflection. However, while you may be reflecting by yourself, you may choose to reflect on both introspective and extrospective matters.

Pause

What are your preferred focal points for reflection?

What might your own assumption hunting illuminate?

VEHICLES FOR REFLECTION

Once you have created the space to reflect and you have a sense of what you are seeking to reflect upon, the next question is "how"? The working assumption is that journalling can be beneficial for coaches and is supported by some of the client-oriented research in the therapeutic community (Lepore and Smyth, 2002). Indeed, most coaching schools endorse this stance. This perspective is also supported by a number of authors. Hay (2007) describes how journal writing offers a way of looking at a body of work, as we can return and examine the evidence for patterns and themes that might inform what we take to supervision. Moon (2004) echoes this, describing how writing links to frontal lobe activity increasing meta-cognition, problem solving and deeper thinking. Bassot (2016) also explains how learning more about the self can be achieved through writing reflective accounts. Frieman (2015) gives further weight to journalling, suggesting that handwritten work is critical to reflective practice, as it is more effective than keyboard practices.

Bassot (2016) observes that journalling is positioned as the primary doctrine of how we reflect. It is interesting that much of the literature on reflective practice is given over to the pursuit of such a specific activity. What about the many coaches who may not enjoy writing and find that journalling halts rather than liberates their thinking? What about the coaches who may not have the capacity for written language? Does this mean their personalised approach to reflection is relegated below that of the written account? One might argue for general equality and question the ethics of emphasising one approach as the single most effective way to reflect.

The idea of creative reflection exists in other professions. For example, Tadayon and Afhami (2016) found evidence that doodling stimulates both right and left brain, improving learning and retention in Junior High School students. They explain how doodling stimulates the visual cortex; enabling the doodler to create mental images and solve problems in innovative ways. They go on to say that this triggers the unconscious mind while keeping the conscious activated. Furthermore, Simmons (2016) noted that there are strong associations between creative techniques and stress reduction, as they engage the parasympathetic nervous system, acting as a parachute within our bodies, reducing stress and inducing wellbeing.

More recent literature is now recognising creativity as a vehicle to unwrap our reflections. Kirkman and Brownhill (2020) highlight the need for reflectors to develop unique ways that hold personal interpretation, as these are more likely to be an authentic account of our experiences. They emphasise the need for us to "*attend to explicit*" and "*tacit knowing,*" considering our minds and bodies as useful data in the practice of reflection. They developed the

"Reflective Shapes Approach" where practitioners combine responses to reflective questions within the mark-making of a bespoke two-dimensional shape (see pages 85–87). They found that the lack of conformity enabled disruptive thinking and supported the practitioner to grapple with more challenging concepts as part of their practice. One of Butler's (2022) six domains is entitled the "Art of Self-Reflection" and refers to the vehicle, tool and/or technique chosen for independent reflective practice. Her research illustrated that practitioners become increasingly more creative as they move through the reflective orientations. Patterson's (2015) research highlights how leaders also derive benefit from reflection, and that they described the process as a creative act, freeing potential and bringing new possibilities for the leaders and their stakeholders.

The research stated above encourages us to embrace creative approaches, connecting mind, body and emotions. From a diversity perspective, these approaches help to bridge language and culture barriers, moving away from conformity and stepping into freedom of expression in a psychologically safe environment. Kirkman and Brownhill (2020) position reflective practice as a creative act to develop professional understanding. While that creative act may be achieved through the written word, journalling is not the only method of reflection available to us. There is room for a range of vehicles to optimise independent reflection. The chapters that follow, invite you to try out new and creative ways to get to know yourself, your practice and the field in which you work, in deeper and more meaningful ways.

Pause

What assumptions do you have about vehicles for reflection?

Where did you learn them?

What do you feel inclined to keep? What is it time to let go of?

STRENGTHENING OUR REFLECTIVE MUSCLE

In experimenting with a range of reflective experiences, a clearer sense of our reflective preferences is likely to emerge. Through creating a regular reflective habit a greater sense of mastery may also be accomplished. To benchmark progress and to become proactive in our development, two models are offered which consider how reflective maturity evolves.

Biggs and Collis (1982), developed the SOLO taxonomy describing five levels of the Structure of the Observed Learning Outcome:

1   Pre-structural: Where we misunderstand a point completely
2   Uni-structural: Where we understand a single basic element
3   Multi-structural: Where we understand several separate elements
4   Relational: Where we begin to understand and integrate concepts
5   Extended Abstraction: Where we build and generate thoughts from wider and alternative perspectives

Building on this work, Moon (2004) remarked on how it could be extended to mirror reflections of increasing complexity. Both Moon and Biggs & Collis come from the education field, so in Figure 1.5, we have used their principles to illustrate a coaching practitioner's view of reflection at each level of the SOLO Taxonomy. These levels offer clues as to how we might stretch our reflective practice one step at a time.

Butler's (2022) research specifically explored self-reflection in coaches. She identifies four broad areas of reflective maturity, each highlighting a different focus of attention or "orientation" when the coach engages in reflection.

1   Technical Model Oriented – reflection is oriented towards models and techniques for coaching
2   Critical Emotional Oriented – reflection is oriented towards models and skill (toolbox)
3   Dynamic Relational Oriented – reflection is oriented towards thoughts, emotions and relationships
4   Eclectic Systemic Oriented – reflection is oriented towards abstract, complex processing and filtering

Within each of these areas, she articulates six domains of self-reflection (see Figure 1.6).

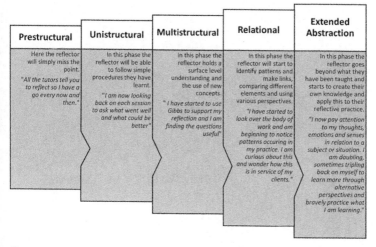

Prestructural	Unistructural	Multistructural	Relational	Extended Abstraction
Here the reflector will simply miss the point. "All the tutors tell you to reflect so I have a go every now and then."	In this phase the reflector will be able to follow simple procedures they have learnt. "I am now looking back on each session to ask what went well and what could be better"	In this phase the reflector holds a surface level understanding and the use of new concepts. "I have started to use Gibbs to support my reflection and I am finding the questions useful"	In this phase the reflector will start to identify patterns and make links, comparing different elements and using various perspectives. "I have started to look over the body of work and am beginning to notice patterns occuring in my practice. I am curious about this and wonder how this is in service of my clients."	In this phase the reflector goes beyond what they have been taught and starts to create their own knowledge and apply this to their reflective practice. "I now pay attention to my thoughts, emotions and senses in relation to a subject or situation. I am doubling, sometimes tripling back on myself to learn more through alternative perspectives and bravely practice what I am learning."

Figure 1.5 SOLO taxonomy of learning applied to coaching reflection examples

Figure 1.7 details how these domains mature through each reflective orientation. While her findings are presented as a sequential model, she noticed that coaches flexed in and out of the different levels of depth, depending on context. For example, an early career coach may self-reflect on the model they used, asking whether they had used it well and whether there may be room for improvement (Technical Model Orientated); and that same coach may also reflect on what they have avoided in a session, for example collusion and bias (Critical Emotional Orientated). Although the sample size is small this research identifies that reflection in action (Schön, 1983) only appears in "eclectic systemic oriented." This lends weight to the idea that reflection in action is only possible when the practitioner is experienced in other forms of reflection.

Reference notes:

1   Argyris (1976)
2   Hawkins and Shohet (2012)
3   Torbert (1999)
4   Biggs and Collis (1982)

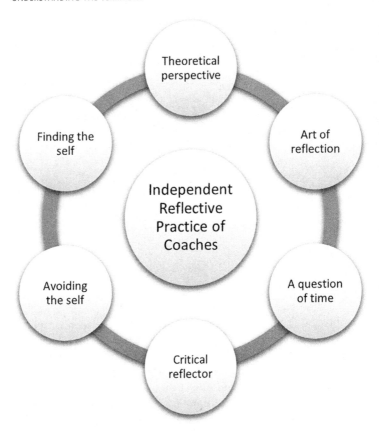

Figure 1.6 Six domains of independent reflective practice (Butler, 2022)

5   Moon (2004)
6   Megginson and Clutterbuck (2009)
7   Mezirow (1998)
8   Schön (1983)
9   Thompson and Thompson (2018)
10   Ghaye (2010)

This framework might enable coaches to understand their current approach to independent reflective practice and in turn highlight new aspects to employ in their development. However,

Technical Model Orientated	Critical Emotional Orientated	Dynamic Relational Orientated	Eclectic Systemic Orientated
Theorectical Perspective - Unstructured, single learning loop[1]	**Theorectical Perspective** - Some links to theory, single/double learning loop[1]	**Theorectical Perspective** - Links to theory, double learning loop[1]	**Theorectical Perspective** - Alternative perspectives (e.g. 7 Eyed Model[2]) - Triple Learning Loop[3]
Art - Journal	**Art** - Mixed written media	**Art** - A range of media used, though it is non-directional and unselective	**Art** - Selective, directive and connected
Time - Reflection On-Action	**Time** - Reflection For-Action and On-Action	**Time** - Reflection For-Action, On-Action. With-Action	**Time** - Reflection For-Action, In-Action, On-Action, With-Action
Professional Importance - Based on teaching and learning	**Professional Importance** - Based on teaching and learning	**Professional Importance** - For supervision and practice development	**Professional Importance** - Links to SR supervision, accreditation
Critical Reflector - Thoughts are towards models and techniques for coaching	**Critical Reflector** - Thoughts are towards models and skill (toolbox)	**Critical Reflector** - Reflects on thoughts, emotionas and relationships	**Critical Reflector** - Abstract, complexed, processing and filtering
Avoiding the Self - Avoids technical e.g. interruptions and advice	**Avoiding the Self** - Avoids relational s e.g. collusion, bias	**Avoiding the Self** - Avoids dynamics s e.g. transference and projection	**Avoiding the Self** - Deliberately seeks that which we avoid
Finding Self - The focus is on their own thoughts	**Finding Self** - The focus is on their own thoughts and emotions	**Finding Self** -The focus is on their own thoughts, emotions and client feedback	**Finding Self** - The focus is on embodiment and they employ a whole system approach. The describe liberation and being connected to self, others and universe

Figure 1.7 Reflective orientations (Butler, 2022)

Butler (2022) emphasises how this is intended as a framework for reflection, learning and growth rather than rubric to measure competency.

It can be tempting to imagine that in knowing these models we will automatically deepen our reflections. While they offer the opportunity for greater evaluation and the frameworks help us pose different questions to reflect upon, the depth and maturity of reflection is most likely to emerge through a persistent and iterative practice. To paraphrase the 12th century poet Dante, "there's no way around it, only through."

Pause

How would you describe the maturity of your reflective practice?

How might you use these taxonomies to evaluate and develop how you use reflection?

CONCLUSION

While this book encourages the practitioner to broaden their repertoire of independent reflective practice, Turner and Lucas (2022) encourages us to see the iterative, dynamic, and sometimes anarchic relationship between independent reflection and other forms of reflective practice. They propose that the practitioner loops and iterates amongst different types of reflection, with different types of reflective partners, on different scopes of content and where overtime the maturity of the reflector builds. So, while reflective maturity is unlikely to be maximised purely through independent reflection, what follows offers a place from which to start.

Pause

How will you leverage both your independent reflection and your reflection with others?

REFERENCES

Argyris, C. (1976) 'Single-Loop and Double-Loop Models in Research on Decision Making', *Administrative Science Quarterly*, 21(3), pp. 363–375.

Bachkirova, T., Jackson, P., Henning, C. and Moral, M. (2020) 'Supervision in Coaching: Systematic Literature Review', *International Coaching Psychology Review*, 15(2), pp. 31–53.

Bassot, B. (2016) *The Reflective Practitioner Guide – An Interdisciplinary Approach to Critical Reflection*. London: Routledge.

Biggs, J. and Collis, K. (1982) *Educational Psychology Series, Evaluating the Quality of Learning, The SOLO Taxonomy (Structure of the Observed Learning Outcome)*. London: Academic Press Incorporated.

Broadwell, M. M. (1969) 'Teaching for Learning (XVI)', *The Gospel Guardian*, 20(41), pp. 1–3.

Brookfield, S. D. (2016) 'Becoming a Critically Reflective Teacher', in Bassot, B. (ed.) *The Reflective Practice Guide: An Interdisciplinary Approach to Critical Reflection*. London: Routledge.

Butler, H. (2022) *Exploring the Experience of Self-Reflection and the Impact Self-Reflection Has on Coaching Practice: A Grounded Approach*. MSc Dissertation. Sheffield Hallam University.

Cooperrider, D. L. and Whitney, D. (2000) 'A Positive Revolution in Change: Appreciative Inquiry', in Golembiewski, R. T. (ed.) *Handbook of Organizational Behavior, Revised and Expanded (Public Administration and Public Policy) 2nd Edition.* US: Routledge, pp. 611–630.

Dante, A. (2008) 'Inferno', *The Divine Comedy (Oxford World's Classics).* Oxford: Oxford University Press, pp. 45–196.

Dehlin, M. and Lundh, L. G. (2018) 'Compassion Fatigue and Compassion Satisfaction Among Psychologists: Can Supervision and a Reflective Stance Be of Help?' *Journal for Person-Oriented Research,* 4(2), pp. 95–107.

Frieman, M. (2015) 'A 'Cognitive Turn' in Creative Writing – Cognition, Body and Imagination', *New Writing – The International Journal for the Practice and Theory of Creative Writing,* 12(2), pp. 127–142.

George, A. (2021) 'Phronesis as Reflection', *Philosophy of Coaching: An International Journal,* 6(2), pp. 7–21.

Ghaye, T. (2010) *Teaching and Learning Through Reflective Practice, A Practical Guide.* Abingdon: Routledge.

Gibbs, G. (1988) *Learning by Doing: A Guide to Teaching and Learning Methods.* Oxford: Oxford Brookes University.

Graßmann, C. and Schermuly, C. C. (2018) 'The Role of Neuroticism and Supervision in the Relationship Between Negative Effects for Clients and Novice Coaches', *Coaching: An International Journal of Theory, Research and Practice,* 11(1), pp. 74–88.

Hawkins, P. and Shohet, R. (2012). *Supervision in the Helping Professions (Supervision in Context).* London: Open University Press.

Hay, J. (2007) *Reflective Practice and Supervision for Coaches.* Maidenhead: Open University Press.

Hicks, J. S. and Townsend, N. W. (2002). *The U.S. Army War College: Military Education in a Democracy.* US: Temple University Press.

King, P. M. and Kitchener, K. S. (1994) *Developing Reflective Judgment: Understanding and Promoting Intellectual Growth and Critical Thinking in Adolescents and Adults.* San Francisco: Jossey-Bass.

Kirkman, P. and Brownhill, S. (2020) 'Refining Professional Knowing as a Creative Practice: Towards a Framework for Self-Reflective Shapes and Novel Approach to Refelction', *Reflective Practice – International and Multidiciplinary Perspectives,* 21(1), pp. 94–109.

Lepore, S. J. and Smyth J. M. (2002) *The Writing Cure: How Expressive Writing Promotes Health and Emotional Well-Being.* American Psychological Association.

Megginson, D. and Clutterbuck, D. (2009) *Further Techniques for Coaching and Mentoring.* Oxford: Butterworth Heinemann.

Mezirow, J. (1998) 'On Critical Reflection', *Adult Education Quarterly,* 48(3), pp. 185–198.

Moon, J. (2004) *A Handbook of Reflective and Experiential Learning: Theory*. New York: Taylor and Francis.

Patterson, E. (2015). 'What Are Leaders' Experiences of Reflection?' What Leaders and Leadership Developers Need to Know From the Findings of an Exploratory Research Study', Reflective Practice, 16(5), pp. 636–651.

Proctor, B. (1986) 'Supervision: A Co-operative Exercise in Accountability' in Marken, M. and Payne, M. (eds.) *Enabling and Ensuring*. Leicester, UK: Leicester National Youth Bureau and Council for Education and Training in Youth and Community Work, pp. 21–23.

Schön, D. (1983) *The Reflective Practitioner: How Professionals Think in Action*. London: Routledge.

Simmons, M. (2016) *Keep Calm and Doodle on: A Relationship Between Doodling and Stress Reduction*. Notre Dame de Namur University.

Tadayon, M. and Afhami, R. (2016) 'Doodling Effects on Junior High School Students' Learning', *The International Journal of Art & Design Education*, 36(1), pp. 118–125.

Thompson, S. and Thompson, N. (2018) *The Critical Reflective Practitioner*. London: Palgrave.

Torbert, W. R. (1999) 'The Distinctive Questions Developmental Action Inquiry Asks', *Management Learning*, 30(2), pp. 189–206.

Turner, T. and Lucas, M. (2023) 'Spiralling the Field: A Dynamic Model Exploring Reflective Maturity, Reflective Capacity and the Expanding Reflective Field', *International Journal of Evidence-based Coaching and Mentoring*, 21(1), pp. 211–221.

Turner, T., Lucas, M. and Whitaker, C. (2018) *Peer Supervision in Coaching and Mentoring, A Versatile Guide for Reflective Practice*. Abingdon: Routledge.

2

HOW TO DEVELOP YOUR REFLECTIVE HABIT

The purpose of this chapter is to help you create a bespoke approach to your reflective practice. My own journey has not been a straight line. It has been more like a murmuration; it has ebbed, flowed, split, re-formed and generally danced its way through my professional life. There is a restlessness, a sense of perpetual motion in my journey as I search for "the thing" that will help sustain my reflective habit. Occasionally I find a place to settle to rest and consolidate … then almost inevitably, I take off again on the next wave of exploration, curious to discover what will open up my awareness. In my experience the only way to make progress is to dive in and discover what is and is not effective … for you.

My sense is that developing the reflective habit has seven components: space, content, process, structure, purpose, reinforcement and review. What follows therefore is guidance to experiment with each of these. I believe that a sustainable reason for engaging in reflection will arise from your visceral experiences rather than your intellectual rationale for it. So, until you are making headway on the first four experiments, your sense of purpose may not have the traction it deserves. However, the choice of when you do what, is entirely yours.

1 PREPARATORY EXPERIMENT (SPACE): IDENTIFYING PROTECTED TIME

Let's start with the practical question of when you will engage in reflection. You may find it useful to reflect immediately after a

DOI: 10.4324/9781003311188-3

session. If you have control over your diary, and you enjoy taking a disciplined approach, or you like to have a sense if completion … then this might suit you. Alternatively, you may find it helpful to let things settle a little to see what rises to the top. This is what happens most naturally for me. As you experiment, try out both strategies to see how the timing improves or detracts from the quality of your reflections. Importantly, as we explored in more detail in Chapter 1 – remember that reflective practice involves more than looking back (reflecting) on our coaching practice. It is equally important to use the space to think ahead, as one of my supervisees calls it, "pre-flection." This may help break the assumption that we "should" reflect after a client session – in fact we can choose any time and space that will help us look both forwards and backwards.

Consider:

- How much time do I want to commit to developing the reflective habit?
- When in my day, week, month could I find this time?
- Where in your schedule can you find slots where you are less likely to be distracted by other activities?

The "when" is often linked to the "where" as it's useful to clarify what locations will help you do your best reflective work. Finding a quiet corner in a city can be challenging and the need to get to your next appointment might compete with the desire to have a more reflective energy. Perhaps it is more realistic to include time for reflection when you are having a desk day? However, also consider whether the task-oriented energy for your administration is congruent with your energy for reflection.

I had a key "aha moment" when I realised it was legitimate to reflect somewhere other than at my desk, with a pen and paper in hand. My daily commute provided me with an opportunity to "wind up" and "wind down." I walk my dogs twice daily, we live by the sea, so sitting on a bench watching the world go by also gives me space at the start and end of the day. Helpfully, these are times when it is difficult to do much else.

I would encourage you to deliberately construct a space that honours the importance of reflection. For example, one of the Reflective Practice Space participants moved to a cosy corner of her house and lit some candles – it generated a sense of indulgence, because she knew that time to reflect was precious. Be open to which place will serve you best, it may not be where you anticipate. I have a lovely grey leather swivel armchair in my office. It's the place I curl up with a book. I assumed this would also be a good location for reflection. However, I discovered that while it's a comfy place to spend time absorbing other people's ideas, it doesn't help me process my own thoughts.

Consider:

- Where do you tend to "mull over" things?
- Where will your reflective space be?
- How might you signal for yourself, that you are entering into a different mindset as well as a different space?

2 PREPARATORY EXPERIMENT (CONTENT): DETERMINING WHAT TO REFLECT UPON

As you might imagine, there is no right answer to what you choose to reflect upon. However, if you already engage in professional supervision, you might replicate your preparation for that, with your independent reflective practice. Here are some of the routes into the content for reflection which I suggest to my supervisees:

1   What's on top? That is, when you look back over the last day, week or month – what draws your attention?

- If nothing seems remarkable, consider moments that seemed to flow well, or conversely moments that seemed a bit sticky

2   What's coming up that you want to prepare for? [See pages 8–10 for an explanation of how reflection can be future focused]

3   Who is on your client list?

- If you simply create a list of your clients from memory – it can be interesting to see in what order they come to mind. As you identify each of them, pause to see if there is any "grit" which might merit further exploration. Once the list is completed, check back to your formal client log – who did you miss? What might that tell you?

4   What is the focus of your current professional development agenda?

- Which of the more technical elements of your practice do you want to improve upon? Consider which of your clients have provided opportunities to hone that element – did you maximise or minimise that opportunity?

5   What do you notice about what there is to reflect upon?

- This can be a useful question to consider when you feel that there is nothing to work with. Why might that be? Could you have plateaued in your practice? Are you taking on the right kind of clients? Are there other areas of your life that are demanding your energy and attention? How are you managing your own self-care?
- By contrast it's a useful question to consider when there is almost too much to reflect upon. Perhaps you are taking on too much? Or a longstanding source of client work is going through a peak in their organisation? Perhaps there are some personal development issues that need attention first?

Chapter 1 included some of the literature about reflective practice. Bassot (2016) suggests that our daily meanderings are not reflective practice. Nonetheless, in my experience these meanderings are significant and useful. On occasion I will notice that something is "occupying me" – it might be a past session, or it might be the thought of an upcoming session. Something in me knows this matter needs further exploration. I make a mental note which I return to when I have some quality reflective time.

When I am preparing for my next supervision, and nothing seems pressing, I will often engage in the client list activity (3) above.

Personally, I like to use post it notes, marking out one for each client. In addition to noticing the sequencing of the clients, I will often create a constellation map. I place a sticky note for myself and then consider where each of the clients are in the relational space around me. This helps to counter the recency effect of who I saw and when, focusing my attention on how it is to be with each person. Almost always this generates a question or noticing for further reflection.

For those who are mature practitioners it can be tempting to dismiss considerations around technical proficiency. However, while my enthusiasm for reviewing a competency matrix is low, I notice that each time I send my coach or supervision bio to a potential new client, I tweak it. Therefore, when I take approach (4) above, I do so from a coaching signature stance. How might I refine the articulation of my professional brand? What CPD have I done recently and how might I integrate that into the description of my practice? What used to be part of my coaching approach which I now hold less tightly, or have perhaps let go of?

3 PREPARATORY EXPERIMENT (PROCESS): DECIDING WHICH REFLECTIVE PROMPTS TO WORK WITH

This book is organised according to processing style. So, consider what you already know about how you like to learn and how you process information. Leverage this knowledge as a route into developing your reflective habit. If you are not sure about your processing preference, then there are some online tests that may help (see resources page 37).

Consider:

- What's your processing preference?

Where you have a clear preference then, perhaps start in the corresponding section. The range of prompts provided offer a variety of cues within a single preference. So, for example, visual prompts utilise photography, cartoons, drawings, optical illusions and videos.

Where your preference is unknown or unclear, you are free to start experimenting in any section, bringing an open mind. Given there are 12 prompts in each section, perhaps use them sequentially, alternatively flick through and land randomly on a page. At the head of each prompt there is a table which suggests what it might be useful for. So, if you already know the content or focus for your reflection, this might also help you decide.

Consider:

• What's your experimentation methodology – emergent or targeted or something else?

In the Reflective Practice Space sessions, I have noticed that a reflective prompt which appeals to one person irritates another. Additionally, our preferences seem to be fickle. The same prompt which engaged us last time, might disengage us the next. Trust your in-the-moment response, it holds information. You may notice that you feel open to the exercise and naturally seek to continue. Alternatively, you may feel inclined to turn away. Should you choose to, you could challenge yourself to stay with the discomfort. It is also possible that the prompt has no impact. While this could mean that the exercise lacks utility for you, pause before you reject your experience. Perhaps emptiness, numbness, or disengagement could be pertinent to you or to your clients.

Consider:

• What features feel important as you build your reflective practice repertoire? Depth or breadth? Ease or challenge? Familiar or novel?

This whole experiment is an opportunity to learn about how you are learning. Perhaps you are curious to know what your reflections will produce. Perhaps you will be able to observe yourself in reflection, noticing your responses to the different reflective prompts? Perhaps you will be interested to watch how the whole experiment is unfolding?

Consider:

- Where is the focus of your curiosity?

Over time I hope that you discover which kind of reflective prompts have impact for you. However, if your reflections are becoming habituated, this could be a signal that it is timely to experiment more courageously so that you can extend your reflective repertoire.

4 PREPARATORY EXPERIMENT (STRUCTURE): ORGANISING YOUR REFLECTIVE ACTIVITY

In keeping with the theme of this book, I hope you will find a way of structuring your space in a way that is uniquely yours. By way of provocation, the structure offered in (Figure 2.1) is based on the one-hour Reflective Practice Space sessions, you may choose to start with a shorter amount of time, simply adjust the timings to suit.

5 PREPARATORY EXPERIMENT (PURPOSE): CLARIFYING WHY YOU WANT TO DEVELOP YOUR REFLECTIVE HABIT

As mentioned above, until you have immersed yourself in reflective activities and had some measure of success it can be hard to know "why" a reflective habit will serve you. Intellectually you may know that reflection mirrors good practice in the helping professions, but what will it mean for you?

One of the features of (my) coach supervision is that it is less goal oriented than (my) coaching, and more exploratory (see Lucas, 2017). When practitioners come to supervision, they often know that something needs attention. Some describe it as a "niggle" that keeps surfacing, some describe it as an "itch" that needs to be scratched. Rarely do people know what exploring the niggle, or itch will yield – it feels impossible to know what their purpose for the session is, other than to settle the niggle or itch. The literature on the purpose for supervision offers a useful framework for considering the purpose for your independent reflective practice. Here I use the framework developed by the counsellor, Brigid Proctor, in 1986.

Step	Description and explanation
Step 1: Clear the space with 10 minutes of mindfulness practice.	This creates separation from the matter of the moment and allows you to step back and consider what to put your reflective attention to. In the introduction to each section there is an exercise designed to help you attune to a particular processing preference. Alternatively, you could use a more familiar meditative practice. For those who are tempted to dive right in, remember that taking a mindful moment, to place your feet on the floor, and to take a couple of slow and deep breaths, can serve you well.
Step 2: Consider where you want to place your reflective attention.	Perhaps you already know what you will reflect upon, or perhaps you need to take a moment to engage with Experiment 2. This Step might feel task oriented and that it will disrupt the more grounded state evoked from Step 1. However, the order suggested allows your brain to determine what truly deserves attention rather than being hi-jacked by what is demanding your attention right now.
Step 3: Use your chosen template(s).	Perhaps you already know what prompt you want to use for reflection, or perhaps you need to take a moment to engage with Experiment 3. Allocate a chunk of time to engage with the reflective prompt such that you do so in an unhurried fashion; ideally 20 to 30 minutes.
Step 4: Take 10 minutes to capture your learning.	Typically, this involves taking a few notes. Experimenting with different mechanisms is helpful here too. Consider written, digital and voice options, for example, a screen shot or photo of creative work might be more helpful than prose. Sometimes, you'll have specific actions. Keeping your records over time is helpful to those seeking to engage in meta-reflection (more below).
Step 5: Transition away from an introspective energy.	For this final 10 minutes of the Regular Reflective Practice Space, I buddy people up to share their learning. As well as deepening the sense of community, it also helps participants transition out of a deeply introspective space and to re-engage with the world around them. So, consider what would help you make that shift. Perhaps a wander to the kitchen for a chit chat with colleagues or family? Perhaps an e-mail to a colleague who can help hold you to account?
Step 6: Reinforcement.	Before moving on to the next thing in your day, take a moment to engage in your chosen method of self appreciation (see Experiment 6).

Figure 2.1 Typical structure of a Reflective Practice Space

Formative purpose

This is about our development as a practitioner. What are our strengths and our development areas? What do we need to integrate, embed or let go of?

Consider:

- Where am I in my journey towards mastery; what needs attention now?

Normative purpose

This is about working in line with good practice and observing the ethical codes of our profession or industry. It's also about congruence between our espoused brand or professional style and the execution of our practice.

Consider:

- What ethical dilemmas do I, or could I, face?
- What are my strategies for managing them?
- How would I check if my community approves of my approach?

Restorative purpose

This is about creating a sense of equilibrium in our energetic response to our work. Perhaps we feel depleted and need to re-charge. Perhaps we feel invincible and need to ground ourselves. Perhaps we feel full and need to off-load. Perhaps we feel a professional loneliness and need to be with another. This function speaks to the notion that we must first care for ourselves if we seek to care for others.

Consider:

- When did I last have a personal stock-take?
- Am I fit to serve my client to the very best of my ability?

In addition, I would add another aspect of purpose, particularly for practitioners who run their own business. For a fuller discussion see Lucas and Larcombe (2016).

Commercial purpose

This is about noticing the inter-connectedness between running a business and delivering to clients. If we are too busy in the delivery, we can lose sight of our business administration or our future pipeline. If we are not busy enough with clients, it can dent our confidence or cause us to take on assignments that we are not ideally placed to deliver.

Consider:

- How much attention do I place to working "in" my business?
- And how much attention do I place to working "on" my business?
- What is the optimum ratio for me?

6 PREPARATORY EXPERIMENT (REINFORCEMENT): HOW WILL YOU CELEBRATE YOUR SUCCESS?

No matter how long you spent in reflection and no matter how many or few insights emerged – the simple fact that you paused to reflect is worthy of recognition.

I get satisfaction by putting a tick through the entry in my paper diary, celebrating that I did indeed reflect when I intended. Alternatively, if it was an impromptu moment, I quite literally add it to my to-do list; just for the satisfaction of striking it through!

Consider:

- As children we might have got a gold star simply for turning up. What's your adult equivalent?

7 PREPARATORY EXPERIMENT (REVIEW): HOW WILL YOU EVALUATE YOUR REFLECTIVE PRACTICE?

However, you define your purpose, it can be helpful to clarify your measures of progress and of success. Remember to set an appreciative frame for your evaluations. If you currently do nothing, then protecting 10 minutes per week is great first step. Embedding new habits takes time. Be prepared to start small and then build on this.

Consider:

- What do you know about how you have formed new habits in other areas of your life?
- How can you transfer that knowledge in service of your reflective practice?
- What do you notice about your intentions to reflect?
- When you deliver on your intentions, what does that tell you about what you need to include in your habit?
- When you don't do what you intended, what do you do instead?
- How able are you to hold yourself to account, or do you need a buddy to be accountable to?
- How do you savour when things go well and how do you find self-compassion when they don't?

So far, this experiment has been oriented towards the reflection you do alone; however, reflective practice is much broader than this. Practitioners also reflect with peers and professional supervisors, perhaps individually or as part of a group. So, on a regular basis it can be helpful to look at your whole portfolio of reflective moments.

Consider:

- What is the range of my reflective practice and how does each element feed or complement the others?
- What are my habits in reflective practice – how do they serve me; how do they limit me? How do they serve or minimise my client's needs?
- Who am I as a reflective practitioner? Do I show up similarly or differently when I reflect with myself, when with another or with others?
- What might all of this mean for how I organise my reflective practice in future?

There are a number of authors who discuss the concept of coach maturity, for example, Hawkins and Smith (2006) or Megginson and Clutterbuck (2009). It is therefore reasonable to assume that the skill of reflective practice may also be viewed as a developmental journey. In Chapter 1 the SOLO taxonomy of Biggs and Collis (1982) and the Reflective Orientations of Butler (2022) offer frameworks for reviewing the nature of our reflections.

Consider:

- How do I evaluate the maturity of my client practice? To what extent can I apply this approach to my reflective practice?
- Which of the models in Chapter 2 resonate; how might I use those frameworks to review the quality of my reflections?
- What does this review evoke in my head, my heart and my soul?
- What does all of this mean for how I evolve my reflective practice in the next year?

8 THE OPPORTUNITY FOR META-REFLECTION

No matter how you manage your experimentation, my hope is that your chosen individual reflection activities will help you see more than you did at the time and contribute to improving your professional practice. However, there is more learning available to you through some meta-reflection. Where you have made a record of your reflections, you could then analyse what themes or patterns are held within.

Consider:

- What are you discovering about your preferred processing style for reflection?
- What are you noticing about the topics that you routinely reflect upon – what do they have in common? For example, do they tend to be about your performance?

Your relationships? Your organisational context? The wider world? If you are familiar with the Hawkins and Smith (2006) seven-eyed model, this can be a good framework to observe what's been included and what might have been missed

- What do you notice now that is absent from your reflections? If this is tricky, enlist the support of a trusted other – they may be able to spot things that are in your blind spot
- Think about the iceberg analogy (there's more underneath the waterline than above it). Consider what the underlying issues might be, which contributed to the topics you reflected upon – for example, are there hints of low confidence? Arrogance? A lack of purpose? A drive for growth? Again, if you find this tricky, a third party might be a useful thinking partner
- Where do you find yourself getting stuck? And what do you do next? What might this say about your self-awareness, your openness to change, your willingness to ask for help?

As you get ready for your own experimental journey remember my suggestions on how to use this book are just that – suggestions. There is no need to be systematic and there is no need to rush … this is not another task "to do." My invitation is to engage with an immersive experience, playing with the multitude of reflective possibilities on offer. It is only through repeated trial and error, through enlightenment and frustration that you will come to create your very own reflective habit.

RESOURCES

Businessballs (2022) *VAK Learning Styles Self-Assessment Questionnaire*. Available at: https://www.businessballs.com/freepdfmaterials/vak_learning_styles_questionnaire.pdf. (Accessed: 19 September 2022).

HFE (2022) *Learning Style Self-Assessment Questionnaire*. Available at: https://www.hfe.co.uk/learning-styles-questionnaire/. (Accessed: 19 September 2022).

REFERENCES

Bassot, B. (2016) *The Reflective Practitioner Guide – An Interdisciplinary Approach to Critical Reflection*. London: Routledge.

Biggs, J. and Collis, K. (1982) *Educational Psychology Series, Evaluating the Quality of Learning, The SOLO Taxonomy (Structure of the Observed Learning Outcome)*. London: Academic Press Incorporated.

Hawkins, P. and Smith, N. (2006) *Coaching, Mentoring and Organisational Consultancy: Supervision and Development*. Maidenhead: Open University, pp. 157–176.

Lucas, M. (2017) 'From Coach to Coach Supervisor – A Shift in Mind-Set', *International Journal of Evidence Based Coaching and Mentoring*, 15(1), pp. 11–23.

Lucas, M. and Larcombe, A. (2016) 'Helping Independent Coaches Develop Their Business – A Holistic Approach to Supervision or an Opportunity for Supervisors to Exploit Their Position', *International Journal of Mentoring and Coaching*. Professional Section, IX(3), pp. 1–16.

Megginson, D. and Clutterbuck, D. (2009) *Further Techniques for Coaching and Mentoring*. Oxford: Butterworth Heinemann.

Proctor, B. (1986) 'Supervision: A Co-Operative Exercise in Accountability', in Marken, M. and Payne, M. (eds.) *Enabling and Ensuring*. Leicester, UK: Leicester National Youth Bureau and Council for Education and Training in Youth and Community Work, pp. 21–23.

3

COGNITIVE PROMPTS TO AID REFLECTION

AN INTRODUCTION TO REFLECTING WITH COGNITIVE PROMPTS

While the intention of this book is to widen our repertoire of reflective prompts, this section embraces more traditional written journalling ... with a twist. Writing for reflection is often likened to keeping a journal or diary. The assumption is that the reflector writes their narrative in an emergent fashion. There is research which demonstrates that the process of writing aids clarity (Moon, 2004). For some, they will have developed this skill over years of writing their own diaries, for others the idea of filling a blank page causes them to freeze. Here we build on basic written narrative, using a variety of frameworks or forms. The structure offers hooks which can draw out our reflections. Moreover, the ideas contained in these prompts will challenge us to think beyond the questions we naturally ask ourselves.

What is particularly useful about this section, is that each completed prompt acts as a record. By using the same format on multiple occasions, you can then aggregate them and look for meta-themes. If you find this informative, you can adapt the idea to capture the output when using with other types of prompts.

For those who dislike writing or indeed are unable to write, it may be helpful to take the prompts provided and use voice recordings to populate them.

DOI: 10.4324/9781003311188-4

A mindfulness exercise to help you prepare for reflecting with cognitive prompts

- Bring your attention to your breath
- Notice how the air enters your body and how it leaves again
- Engage all of your senses as you breathe and practice a few times to fully connect with the rhythm of your respiration
- Bring to mind a sparkling moment in your personal or professional life. A time when you were truly in form, in flow, or experiencing your maximum intellectual horsepower ....
- On an in-breath, savour that moment, honouring its existence ...
- On an out-breath, place that moment somewhere safe and create more space for what comes next
- Think of another sparkling moment, place your attention to your brain ... can you re-connect with the way in which your synapses were firing ...?
- On an in-breath, savour that moment, honouring its existence ...
- On an out-breath, place that moment somewhere safe and create more space for what comes next
- Repeat the process a few times until you feel confident that you can engage with the reflective prompts leveraging your fullest mental capacity
- Finally, take a couple of nicely resourcing breaths before continuing with the reflective prompts

---

Reference

Moon, J. (2004) *A Handbook of Reflective and Experiential Learning: Theory.* New York: Taylor and Francis.

1 CRITICAL INCIDENT ANALYSIS

Time to Allow	Topics This Could be Specifically Useful For
Preparation time: 2 mins (to access or print the template) Reflection time: 15 minutes or more	Where there has been a "significant moment" in a session, this form can be useful to unpick that moment in greater detail. Particularly useful when you feel surprised by either your own response or your client's response.

Why this framework appealed to me

I was introduced to this reflective process through my Coaching and Mentoring studies at Oxford Brookes. It begins with "log," which gave me permission just to record "what happened," a simple way to start. The title "Critical Incident Analysis" also helped direct my attention to what I might reflect upon. As a trainee coach, there were often sessions that seemed remarkable in some way. Sometimes a mistake on my part, and sometimes because a client experienced an "aha" moment. Importantly, it wasn't always clear how these things came about. The form is an invitation to dig deeper and try to understand why things were the way they were.

I understood that by capturing all these moments and understanding more about them, would help me develop as a coach. This became my "go-to" reflection template throughout my study. However, for those sessions where nothing remarkable happened, this form was less appropriate. This was how I came to develop the Hi's and Lo's matrix (see pages 49–51). In combination, the two forms enabled me to keep a record of almost all my sessions – and formed a good library from which to search for developmental themes.

A pathway for reflection

- Ensure you have a blank template to hand
- Populate the framework in sequence from top to bottom
- Notice which sections are harder than others to complete (that's data)
- Find a balance between pushing your thinking and allowing your thinking to distil …. If you are really struggling to complete a section, perhaps pause and return to it later.
- Before "filing" the template, ensure you have added the information at the top (Figure 3.1)

CRITICAL INCIDENT ANALYSIS - REFLECTION FORM

Date of Event:

Date of Reflection:

LOG: Put the facts of what happened here

DIARY: Articulate your feelings about what happened here

JOURNAL: Analyse what happened bringing in objective data so that you can rationalise and make sense of what happened.

PLAN: Based on reflection and analysis, identify what future action you want to take

Figure 3.1 Critical incident analysis – Reflection form

Reference

Clutterbuck, D., Whitaker, C. and Lucas, M. (2016) *Coaching Supervision: A Practical Guide for Supervisees*. Abingdon: Routledge, p. 164.

2 DEEPENING YOUR REFLECTIVE WRITING

Acknowledgement: Christine K Champion

Time to Allow	Topics This Could be Specifically Useful For
Preparation time: 2 mins (to access or print the template)	Any reflection where you sense there is more beneath the surface than at first appears
Reflection Time: 10 minutes or more	Random reflections where greater clarity could be achieved through leveraging a more structured and objective framework

Why this framework appealed to me

Christine and I developed this framework for a reflective writing workshop for an organisational client when some of their coaches were intending to apply for individual accreditation. In supporting their applications, it seemed that the business report writing they engaged in on a day-to-day basis almost de-skilled them from the more reflective writing required by the professional coaching body.

Taking this approach reminds me of peeling the proverbial onion. I work my way through, layer by layer. With each iteration I start to see more, this fuels more curiosity and further questions. It happens step-by-step, there is no shortcut. I have noticed though, that over time, the way I move through the levels has become more fluid.

A pathway for reflection

- Start by identifying something that merits additional reflective time and effort
- Write just a few sentences in the descriptive column
- Move to the analytical column and consider what prompts or frameworks could be useful

  - Consider

    - The seven-eyed model (Hawkins & Smith, 2006)
    - A competency framework
    - Perceptual positions (I, you, we, other)
    - Identification of strengths

Descriptive (What happened)	Analytical (Sense making)	Reflexive (Personal meaning)
Example: This is what happened and what I would do differently next time. This is a subjective or personal account, it may have a surface or transactional feel.	Example: Focusing in more deliberately on elements that seem key. Bringing a greater granularity and specificity to what you have evidence for and what is absent. Taking a more objective and rational approach to what happened and how.	Example: Slowing down to bring into awareness what might have been out of awareness in the moment of the session. How does what happened sit with your sense of who you are? What threw you off balance and why? What helped you stay centred and how?
Typical question: What happened?	Typical question: How would I categorise what happened?	Typical question: What does what happened say about me?

Figure 3.2 A tabular approach to deepening written reflections

- Deliberately use those prompts to explore what lies beneath your written description
- Before moving to the reflexive column – centre yourself so that you can access a higher and fuller state of awareness
- Return to your analytical writing, slow down further and start to notice what information is arising from your somatic self. Consider the passing of time and how you may have responded in an earlier chapter of your career; comment on any changes you are now noticing in you. Consider how you have come to know what you know now (Figure 3.2).

Reference

Hawkins, P. and Smith, N. (2006) *Coaching, Mentoring and Organisational Consultancy: Supervision and Development*. Maidenhead: Open University, pp. 157–176.

3 COMPETENCY FRAMEWORKS

Time to Allow	Topics This Could be Specifically Useful For
Preparation time: 2 mins (to access or print the template) Reflection time: 60 minutes or more	Identifying areas of strength that you could leverage further Identifying blind spots Creating a competency-based developmental action plan

Why this framework appealed to me

I noticed the potential value of reflecting against a competency framework when applying for coach accreditation. While it required effort, the rigour that it required helped me build a comprehensive development plan.

What became challenging was the disconnect between what I perceived as a strength and the evidence I had. Perhaps because when leveraging a strength, I was operating in "flow." The experience felt good, but my ability to access supporting data was reduced. I considered whether the absence of evidence implied an absence of skill. In my next coaching sessions, I noticed a different intention and energy because I deliberately sought to remain in a consciously competent state.

Figure 3.3 captures the process I used for myself. Working systematically through the columns, it keeps me honest with myself. Where there are gaps, it prompts me to address them in my Continuous Professional Development.

A pathway for reflection

- Download your chosen competency framework (see Resources)
- Shortlist three competencies to review. Ideally one strength,

Competency (from Professional Body)	Interpretation of competency indicators	Confidence Rating (Hi/Med/Lo)	Supporting Evidence	Counter Evidence
Building Relationship (as an example)	Takes a respectful and non-judgemental perspective			
	Creates an atmosphere of trust			
	Uses language appropriate to client and their context			
	Facilitates transparency between client and sponsors			

Figure 3.3 Example self-assessment competency matrix

one development area, and one where you are unsure of your effectiveness

- Add them to the form, putting any detailed indicators into your own words as sub-headings
- Bring to mind a handful of clients. Re-enliven your memory of how they were in the session, for example, how did they look, sound, or move?
- Address the grid column by column. Work quickly and instinctively – if there is clear evidence or counter-evidence, it will appear. If there's a lack of evidence at this stage, move on
- Complete this activity monthly and review what you have done on a quarterly basis. You will probably notice patterns emerging
- Where there is a lack of evidence, be open to three possibilities

  1 You may have delivered on this competency with other clients
  2 You may have been working in unconscious competence
  3 You may not be using this competency … yet

- Where there is counter-evidence, perhaps there is something distinctive about your coaching approach which differs from your professional body. If so, check that this is included in your marketing collateral
- At least once a year, consider how you feel about your self-assessments. Notice where you instinctively took action and where you were inclined to procrastinate. What does that mean for you? Finally, consider which competencies you want to review in the year ahead

Resources

AC (2021) *AC Coaching Competency Framework*. Available at: http://cdn.ymaws.com/www.associationforcoaching.com/resource/resmgr/Accreditation/Accred_General/Coaching_Competency_Framewor.pdf (Accessed: 19 September 2022).

EMCC (2015) *EMCC Global Competence Framework V2*. Available at: http://www.emccuk.org/Common/Uploaded%20files/Resources/EMCC_competencies2021.pdf (Accessed: 19 September 2022).

ICF (2022) *Core Competencies*. Available at: http://www.coaching federation.org.uk/credentialing/icf-core-competencies (Accessed: 19 September 2022).

Reference

Csikszentmihalyi, M. (2009) *Flow: The Psychology of Optimal Experience*. New York: Harper & Row.

4 FOUR PS FOR CONTRACTING

Time to Allow	Topics This Could be Specifically Useful For
Preparation time: 2 mins (to access or print the template)	This is generally useful for those who want to put particular emphasis on reviewing their contracting approach with groups. It is also relevant for individual contracting.
Reflection time: 20 minutes or more	Where a session feels hesitant, or perhaps things are left unsaid – this could be a clue that something has been overlooked in the contract.

Why this framework appealed to me

This framework stems from the thinking of Julie Hay (2007) – who identified the Procedural, Professional and Psychological elements of contracting with a group. At the time many of my clients were from organisational contexts and I noticed, particularly in groups, the potential for the power dynamics in the wider system to surface. I therefore added the fourth P – labelling it Political, creating a quadrant of frames (see Figure 3.4).

I tend to use these quadrants as a mental checklist during in-dividual and group sessions. When I start noticing hesitations or what seem like rehearsals before speaking, I wonder if these are clues that something might have been missed or needs re-visiting in the contract. Of course, the structure also lends itself to deliberately review what level of contracting you have put in place with your client(s).

PROCEDURAL	PROFESSIONAL
Logistics, protocols for time keeping, managing distractions, notice for cancellation, minimum and maximum group number, structure of session, requirement (or not) for preparation, emergent vs turn-taking approaches	• How do we want to behave? • What might support and challenge look like here? • What ethical code will we observe? • What does Diversity, Equality and Inclusion mean in this context?
PSYCHOLOGICAL	**POLITICAL**
• How human will we be? • How will we handle comparisons with our peers? • What about shame? Competition? • How vulnerable are we prepared to be? • What previous good and bad experiences of coaching/supervision / facilitation do we bring here?	• Who tends to go first? Who waits to be invited to speak? • Who prefers not to bring something? • What "logic" is used when determining the order of who goes when? • What power positions may we wittingly or unwittingly occupy? For example: Who has the most senior "day job" or who has been longest in the group? How will we make this transparent? • What else could get in the way of the work?

Figure 3.4 The four Ps for contracting: Questions to consider

A pathway for reflection

- Ensure you have the quadrant and its questions to hand
- Where you have a sense of which area might need attention, go straight to that category. Alternatively, you could move through the quadrants sequentially
- Notice which elements you have covered comprehensively, this can provide reassurance that you have some firm foundations in place
- Notice which items have been glossed over, and which could benefit from further articulation. Consider what evidence you have that a detailed conversation occurred – for example, if "support and challenge" was mentioned …. how did you clarify that you were talking about the same thing?
- Place particularly candid attention to the Political category – how comprehensive was the conversation about the kind of relationship dynamics which could be in play? Are there still some "elephants in the room"?
- Where you identify an omission, consider how you might mitigate this

Reference

Hay, J. (2007) *Reflective Practice and Supervision for Coaches.* UK: McGraw-Hill Education.

Further reading

Lucas, M. (2020) 'Contracting Using Four Ps', in Lucas. M. (ed) *101 Coaching Supervision Techniques, Approaches, Enquiries and Experiments.* Abingdon: Routledge, pp. 223–226.

5 HI'S AND LO'S

Time to Allow	Topics This Could be Specifically Useful For
Preparation time: 2 mins (to access or print the template) Reflection time: 10 minutes or more	This is generally useful for those who require a regular record of reflections on their client sessions. Additionally, it can be useful if you leave a session feeling particularly smug or particularly critical as it will help to bring a greater sense of balance.

Why this framework appealed to me

I developed this 2 × 2 matrix (see figure 3.5) when I was studying to become a coach – I wanted a simple structure that I could repeatedly use to capture my reflections on a session. Sometimes it prompted a need to do additional reflection using a more analytical process. But what I liked about it was its simplicity – and the consistent layout allowed me to compare multiple sessions over time so I could spot themes. What did I feel I served my client well? What prompted my internal critic to appear? Where did the focus of my learning gravitate to? And … did I actually implement my action plans!

When supporting other coaches to develop their reflective habits, I often suggest this template as a starter for 10. The simple, yet balanced format, seems to make intuitive sense and general feedback is that it helps the process of reflection seem more accessible.

COACHING SESSION REVIEW FORM

Client: **Session Date:**   **Session No:**

Date of Reflection:

HIGHLIGHTS	LOWLIGHTS
LEARNING	COMMITMENT FOR FUTURE

Figure 3.5 Coaching session review form

A pathway for reflection

- Ensure you have a blank template to hand, either printed or on a device, or simply map the matrix out freehand
- Populate the framework in whichever order your reflections naturally emerge
- Notice which sections are harder than others to complete (that's data)

- Manage your energy to complete as many sections as you can without it feeling tiresome

    - Note: the more sections you comment on, the more balanced your reflections will become

- Before filing the template, ensure you have added the information at the top

Reference

Clutterbuck, D., Whitaker, C. and Lucas, M. (2016) *Coaching Supervision: A Practical Guide for Supervisees*. Abingdon: Routledge, p. 166.

6 NAIKAN

Time to Allow	Topics This Could be Specifically Useful For
Preparation time: 2 mins (to access or print the template) Reflection time: 15 minutes or more	Where you want to understand your relationships more deeply Where you want to both appreciate and hold yourself to account in equal measure

Why this framework appealed to me

I discovered this approach to reflection while researching this book, its simplicity and gentleness spoke to me. According to Krech, 2020 Naikan means "seeing within." The approach was developed by Yoshimoto Ishin, a Japanese businessman and Jodo Shinshu Buddhist. The intention is to deepen our introspection, to be truly grateful for what others give, to help us see the good we are capable of, while also owning any harm we have done (intentionally or not), such that we might identify what repair may be needed.

The approach structures our self-reflection using three questions (see Figure 3.6). You could ask the questions of yourself daily – like a gratitude practice reviewing the day. You could focus on one particular person considering your relationship with them over time. Or you could dedicate a larger amount of time to reviewing

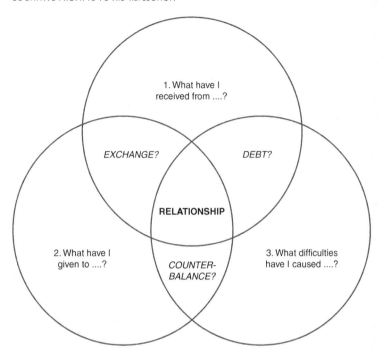

Figure 3.6 Exploring the shape of our relationship using Naikan reflective
        questions

your whole life, in a chronological sequence and asking these
questions of your significant relationships. In the context of professional reflection, the focus on a single relationship over time
seems most useful.

As I explored the three questions with a client in mind, I instinctively drew three interlocking circles. This got me curious
about the size of each circle and the overlap between them.
I identified three concepts (exchange, debt and counter-balance)
that might emerge when we look our three responses side by side.

A pathway for reflection

- Hold a client relationship in your awareness, perhaps remind
  yourself of how you came to work with them and how the
  relationship has unfolded

- Ask yourself following three questions:

  1 What have I received from [NAME]?

    - Consider:

      - What are you grateful for?
      - How easy or difficult do you imagine this was for them?
      - What sacrifices did they make, to do this for me?

  2 What have I given to [NAME}?

    - Consider:

      - What good am I capable of?
      - How freely did I give this?
      - Where does my benevolence stem from?

  3 What difficulties have I caused [NAME]?

    - Consider:

      - What was my intention?
      - How will their wounds heal?
      - What reparatory action do I want to take?

- Perhaps draw the three interlocking circles scaling each one to reflect how much material you have for each … what is the shape of your relationship?
- If you have the appetite, consider how your circles interlock – what do you notice now about the exchange, debt, and counter-balance? Or perhaps the overlapping areas speak of something else to you

Resource

Journal of Japan Naikan Association. Available at: https://www.jstage. jst.go.jp/ (Accessed: 23 August 2022).

Reference

Krech, G. (2002)*Naikan: Gratitude, Grace, and the Japanese Art of Self-reflection*. Naikan Reflection, California: Stone Bridge Press.

Further reading

Fromm, E. (1995) *The Art of Loving*. London: Thorsons.

Wheelis, A. (2006) *The Way We Are*. New York: W. W. Norton & Company.

7 RE-COUNT, RE-LIVE, REVIEW, REVISE, RE-ROUTE, REFRESH

Acknowledgement: Christine Champion

Time to Allow	Topics This Could be Specifically Useful For
Preparation time: 2 mins (to access or print the template) Reflection time: 20 minutes or more	This cycle is useful for any kind of reflection as the process helps bring things into your awareness. Particularly useful when a session is a bit of a blur and you are left unsure of how things really went.

Why this framework appealed to me

When something in my practice doesn't quite go as imagined, my analysis can be quite swift and I almost immediately have a sense of what I should do differently next time. Using this cycle to unpick my reflections helps me to slow down and truly think things through from first principles. Not only does this help me to see more complexity to why things unfolded as they did, in turn this gives me more options of what I might adjust next time around. The cycle originates from Gibbs (1988) Reflective Learning Cycle (see Figure 3.7).

Christine and I developed different labels for each stage, all beginning with "R," to help its memorability, the adapted version can be found in Lucas (2020). So, Describe becomes "re-count"; Feelings become "re-live"; Evaluation becomes "review"; analysis becomes "revise"; conclusion becomes "re-route; and action plan becomes "re-fresh."

A pathway for reflection

• On a large piece of paper (or whiteboard) re-draw the cycle in the middle of the space

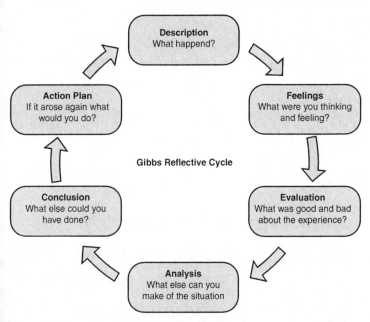

Figure 3.7 The reflective cycle by Gibbs (1988)

- Starting with "Describe," pose each question to yourself noting your responses
- Work your way around the cycle, notice the pace with which you do so … where do you hurry? Where might you linger more fully?
- Use the cycle a few times – typically more information will emerge as you do this. Perhaps use a different coloured pen each time, to track the order of your notes
- Pause and create some distance from your reflections
- Using highlighters identify any connections you now notice across your responses
- Pause again. Look at your notes in the "conclusion" section, notice what action(s) you are inclined to take and what options have you discounted
- Consider what you are learning about your readiness for learning/change

Reference

Gibbs, G. (1988) *Learning by Doing: A Guide to Teaching and Learning Methods*. Oxford: Further Education Unit, Oxford Polytechnic.

Further reading

Honore, C. (2013) *The Slow Fix: Solve Problems, Work Smarter and Live Better in a Fast World*. UK: Collins.

Lucas, M. and Champion, C. K. (2020) 'Reflective Writing', in Lucas. M. (ed) *101 Coaching Supervision Techniques, Approaches, Enquiries and Experiments*. Abingdon: Routledge, pp. 76–79.

8 SENTENCE STEMS FOR JOURNALING

Time to Allow	Topics This Could be Specifically Useful For
Preparation time: None Reflection time: Two minutes or more	Capturing the impact of a session immediately after close Breaking procrastination or identifying a focus for reflection

Why this framework appealed to me

Whenever I was encouraged to journal during coach training, I would "go blank," I had no idea where to start. I realised I needed something to push against and was reminded of psychometrics which used "sentence stems." So, I began with my here-and-now experience and created a sentence stem; things like … "When I reflect back on today's session I … … "or" As I notice my stuckness I … …." This last example is similar to Turner-Vesselago's (2013) notion of freefall writing. More often than not, this gets me off the starting blocks, I can acknowledge my stuckness which then seems to allow me to move on and gives me greater access to more noticing.

As a supervisor, I often invite supervisees to take a minute or two at the end of a session to capture their learning. This approach is documented by Clare Norman (2020) as "Rush Writing" in the 101 book. With my own experience of "journaler's block,"

I tend to offer a sentence stem to get participants started. I like this as I can adapt the sentence stem to mirror the mood or themes within the session, and if I'm lacking inspiration the generic ones are useful too.

A pathway for reflection

- Decide on the time you want to commit to this exercise and set an alarm accordingly
- Create a sentence stem for yourself – or choose a more generic one, for example:
    - What I am noticing now is ….
    - When I reflect on X I feel /notice/imagine/know/sense I …
    - As I pause to reflect I ….
    - As I start this writing I ….
- Write freely without worrying about mistakes or whether it's making sense
- If your writing stalls it can help to keep your pen on the paper and doodle, I sometimes write scribbles in chunks so that they look like words (!) – often a new wave of writing will then flow
- When the time is up stop and notice what learning has emerged and what, if anything, you need to do next

References

Norman, C. (2020) 'Rush Writing', in Lucas. M. (ed) *101 Coaching Supervision Techniques, Approaches, Enquiries and Experiments.* Abingdon: Routledge, pp. 82–84.

Tuner-Vesselago, B. (2013) *Writing Without a Parachute: The Art of Freefall.* US & UK: Jessica Kingsley.

Resource

Writescape (2022) *Seven Tips for Finding Inspiration.* Available at: https://writescape.ca/site/tag/freefall-writing/ (Accessed: 14 September 2022).

9 THE BIG 'R' FRAMEWORK BY PAMELA FAY

Time to Allow	Topics This Could be Specifically Useful For
Preparation time: 2 mins (to access or print the template) Reflection time: 20 minutes or more	When you are wanting to reflect on areas within your practice that are working well. If you are feeling at capacity with work and wish to make choices on how you are spending your time.

Why this framework appealed to me

As a coach, coach supervisor and tutor I often use other models when reflecting on my learning edge in practice. I turn to this model when there are aspects of practice that are working well and I want to reflect on the feeling of flow and to understand more about the reasons behind that. I find this model accessible to use myself and to explain to supervisees too for their reflections.

As a solo practitioner, I welcome the way this model encourages me to reflect outside of myself, inviting me to look for support or to collaborate with the "we" rather than "I" focus. I use this model both in preparation for supervision and when doing reviews of longer time periods too (Figure 3.8).

A pathway for reflection

- Using a pen and paper, write out the four questions over a number of pages, giving yourself space for your responses
- In answering the first question, reflect on the last time in your work when you have felt most fully yourself, working from a place of strength and ease
- Let the pencil or pen write without censoring your answer. Follow your energy
- Bring yourself back to the moment, who was there, what were you doing, how did you feel then and what emerges now for you in your felt sense. What still resonates from that moment?

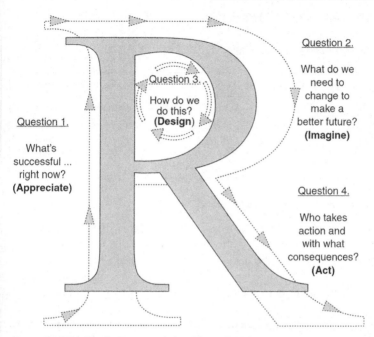

Figure 3.8 The Big R Framework by Ghaye (2010)

- When you have finished answering question one, pause and notice your felt sense now
- Then answer the three remaining questions in succession
- After answering the four questions, pause and note what is within your control and who you need to support you?
- What conversations do you need to have and with who?
- Notice how your energy levels are post reflection
- What is the first step that you can take now?

Reference

Ghaye, T. (2010) *Teaching and Learning Through Reflective Practice, A Practical Guide.* Abingdon: Routledge.

10 THE THREE "WHAT'S"

Acknowledgement: Carol Whitaker

Time to Allow	Topics This Could be Specifically Useful For
Preparation time: 2 mins (to access or print the template) Reflection time: 15 minutes or more	Where you feel sanguine about a moment in a session yet also know the moment holds learning. When you feel ready to do a deep dive on a client matter.

Why this prompt appealed to me

One of my colleagues, who attends the Regular Reflective Practice Space generously shared this template with me as we moved into the second year of the sessions. When I first looked at it, I remember feeling overwhelmed by the density of the questions offered! However, in essence, there are only three "Whats" i.e. three themes for enquiry.

The first invites us to describe what happened as we experienced it. The second asks us to consider what happened in context, to apply our theoretical knowledge and "20:20 hindsight" to the situation. Then finally, we are prompted to consider what action is appropriate now. That felt much more manageable. I reformatted the document into the form provided in Figure 3.9, by creating boxes, it helps to chunk up each set of questions.

In my experience of using it, I rarely answer all the questions posed, rather a couple will seem to draw my attention, and once answered I feel ready to move to the next section. I find it interesting that this approach originated from the nursing professions. Yet simply by substituting the word "patient" with "client" it feels equally pertinent for the coaching community.

A pathway for reflection

- Access the template in an editable format
- Bring a client situation to mind

Enquiry	Questions	Notes
WHAT- Is the situation (Description)	• What did I see? What did I do? • What was my reaction? • What did others do? • What are the key aspects of this situation? • What was good/bad about the situation? • What were the consequences? • What was I trying to achieve?	
SO WHAT - (Theory and Knowledge/ Reflection)	• So what does this tell / teach me / imply / mean about me, my client, others, my attitudes? • So what was going through my mind as I acted? • So what did I base my actions on? • So what other knowledge can I bring to the situation? • So what could / should I have done better? • So what is my new understanding of the situation? • So what broader issues arise from the situation?	
NOW WHAT (Action)	• Now what do I need to do in order to: enhance my knowledge, make things better, stop being stuck, improve patients care, resolve the situation….? • Now what are the implications for you, your colleagues, and the client? • Now what needs to happen to alter the situation? • Now what are you going to do about the situation? • Now what happens if you decide not to alter anything? • Now what might you do differently if faced with a similar situation again? • Now what information do you need to face a similar situation again? • Now what are the best ways of getting further information about the situation should it arise again?	

Figure 3.9 The three "What's" of Rolfe et al. (2001), with example questions

• Cast your eye through the detailed questions, and perhaps use a highlighter to focus in on the one or two questions that you feel drawn to

- Consider each "WHAT" in turn, responding to your selected questions and making notes as you go
- Pause before you conclude and notice which questions you have skipped over – can you answer some of them more easily now?
- Look at the number of actions that you have identified. What will you prioritise on that list?
- If you still have time available ... commence those actions now

Reference

Rolfe, G., Freshwater, D. and Jasper, M. (2001) *Critical Reflection for Nursing and the Helping Professions*. Basingstoke: Palgrave MacMillan.

11 THREE-TWO-ONE

Acknowledgement: Liz Ford

Time to Allow	Topics This Could be Specifically Useful For
Preparation time: None Reflection time: 6 minutes	Identifying themes within a reflection Making meaning from written reflections

Why this framework appealed to me

I was introduced to this framework when Liz wrote the technique for the 101 book. I was immediately drawn to it because it seemed to bring a sense of purpose to a journaling activity. Somehow its structure seemed to reassure me that something good would come out of the exercise. It moves us through description, analysis and action very effectively and swiftly.

I often suggest this activity to capture learning at the end of supervision sessions that I deliver. Both the supervisees and myself engage with it simultaneously, as a private moment. Alternatively, I have used this as a preparatory activity – it helps bring some order when my head is overly cluttered or busy. In the space of 6 minutes, my energy is activated as I find a focus for the session ahead.

The technique can be adapted to your own style. Ford's (2020) original format is phases of 3 minutes, then 2 minutes and then 1 minute. I've noticed that for me it makes sense to structure it 3 then 1 then 2. In the second phase, I tend to highlight keywords rather than continue writing, and this takes less time, whereas the final phase often prompts more thoughts or actions and I welcome the additional time.

A pathway for reflection

- Set your alarm for 3 minutes
- Start writing "whatever comes into your head," don't worry about handwriting, spelling or whether your writing makes sense. Write quickly and constantly – if your writing stalls, doodle with your pen on the paper and trust that more words will come
- Set your alarm for 2 minutes
- Read back through what you have written, then start writing again using a sentence stem like:

  - I am curious about ...
  - I am surprised by ...
  - I feel ...

- Set your alarm for 1 minute
- Write a list of:

  - What you want to take to supervision
  - What you want to take action upon
  - Learnings you have identified

Reference

Ford, L. (2020) '3-2-1: A Reflective Writing Technique', in Lucas. M. (ed) *101 Coaching Supervision Techniques, Approaches, Enquiries and Experiments*. Abingdon: Routledge, pp. 7–9.

12 WRITING IN AND OUT OF THE LABYRINTH

Acknowledgement: Jackee Holder

Time to Allow	Topics This Could be Specifically Useful For
Preparation time: 2 mins (to access or print the template) Reflection time: 10 minutes or more	Any topic where you would either like to drill down further or alternatively where you would like to widen out further. Also useful to combine with Sentence Stems, when finding it hard to begin your reflective activity (see pages x-y)

Why this framework appealed to me

Writing within this interesting shape signposted that I was doing something different to other forms of written communication. The Labyrinth was designed by Jackee Holder (2011) and her suggestion is that we "work inwards to the centre" or "work from the centre outwards." Almost instinctively I noticed the former made me more granular and the latter more expansive (Figures 3.10 and 3.11).

Figure 3.10 Writing in the labyrinth

Figure 3.11 Writing out the labyrinth

Writing the labyrinth highlighted my tendency to rush – I got annoyed that turning the page slowed me down. In noticing my annoyance, I had to chuckle at myself, what was so important about getting to the end? Now, when I spot myself rushing, I deliberately slow down. When I savour my writings, I can notice more about how my thoughts are unfolding. Moving the paper also encourages me to change my perspective prompting me to consider how the situation may appear to others.

Note: This can also be used as a kinaesthetic prompt, simply trace your finger around the maze as you reflect.

A pathway for reflection

- Pick a labyrinth you'd like to use (see resources)
- Decide which direction you want to go – do you want to become more introspective and granular (towards the centre) or do you want to broaden your perspective (from the centre outwards)

- Perhaps you have a question in your mind, perhaps not. Either can bring value – so just start
- Continue until you reach the centre/edge of the maze and then stop. Or set an alarm so that you limit or expand the time taken
- If you find yourself in flow, complete the maze multiple times in the same direction – like peeling or constructing the layers of an onion
- When you reach an end point – consider if you have "enough," or if you remain curious, perhaps work with a maze in the opposite direction

Resource

Holder, J. (2011) *Writing the Labyrinth*. Available at: www.jackeeholder.com/wp-content/uploads/2015/06/Writing-the-labyrinth-April15.pdf (Accessed: 19 September 2022).

References

Holder, J. (2013) *49 Ways to Write Yourself Well: The Science and Wisdom of Reflective Writing and Journaling*. Brighton: Stepbeach Press.

Holder, J. (2020) 'Writing the labyrinth', in Lucas. M. (ed) *101 Coaching Supervision Techniques, Approaches, Enquiries and Experiments*. Abingdon: Routledge, pp. 119–122.

Anecdotes from practitioners using cognitive prompts

Critical incident analysis – Reflective learning form

What shifted as a result of the exercise?

I used this form when I noticed fleeting moments where a client would sometimes frown or pull a face. Because they were quite fleeting my attention moved elsewhere. I started to record what I saw, in doing so I noticed this happened when they were describing certain instances. I wondered if there was a pattern, and then thinking about this, I recalled other occasions too. This prompted me to offer the client some quite specific feedback. Until then they were unaware that they did this. We explored this further, it proved enlightening for them and for me.

How did you feel about the reflective experience?

I first came across Critical Incident Analysis when studying for a coaching qualification as a way of documenting my reflections, it was in a longer format. The form seemed to demand that I start with I start at the top. This caused a form of writer's block, inhibiting my recording of the session. When attending the Reflective Practice Space, I did so "under my own steam" somehow this encouraged me to start at any point, I felt as though I could complete the other boxes in any order I wished. This fired my curiosity and creativeness and helped me find insights and patterns that were not obvious before. When I was reflecting because I wanted to, I was able to get a flow of writing and work deeper.

RPS Participant, Coach and Coach Supervisor, July 2021

Three-Two-One

What shifted as a result of the exercise?

The exercise challenged me to stop writing *about* the situation and the players at 3 minutes in, to notice what I was noticing for the next 2 minutes, which took me to another level of depth and empathy. The last minute gave me immediate resolution and as a result, I was able to record a 3-minute video to send out to the players as soon as I finished the reflection. So in less than 10 minutes, an annoying situation was completely turned around into a positive.

How did you feel about the reflective experience?

Rush writing is a favourite reflective practice for me, so this exercise felt like "home." I had watched Brene Brown's Empathy video beforehand, so the two in combo were useful partners.

Clare Norman, Coach, Coach Supervisor, Master Mentor Coach

4

VISUAL PROMPTS TO AID REFLECTION

AN INTRODUCTION TO REFLECTING WITH VISUAL PROMPTS

Most of us will be familiar with the phrase "a picture is worth a thousand words" and for those who have a visual processing preference, this is undoubtedly true. As the Russian writer Ivan Turgenev purportedly wrote in 1861, "The drawing shows me at one glance what might be spread over ten pages in a book."

In the exercises that follow, we have considered a variety of visual prompts – photographs, drawings, videos and abstract images. Typically, we offer an example of a visual prompt within the text. The reproduction is restricted to greyscale which reduces the visual impact, so in the resource section we signpost you to additional materials which can be viewed in technicolour. We hope these examples provide inspiration and that you will continue to build your own visual library from the wealth of materials that are available elsewhere.

A mindfulness exercise to help you reflect using visual prompts

- Position yourself near a window
- Bring your attention to your breath
- Notice how the air enters your body and how it leaves again
- Place your eyes gently on the outside world, begin to notice the different features in your field of view
- Practice breathing such that you are able to both absorb what you can see and keep your attention on your breath

---

DOI: 10.4324/9781003311188-5

- Open your mind to what your eyes connect with, see beyond an object's function to appreciate its structure, form, texture and perhaps its movement
- Should you start to "think" about what an object is, gently place your attention back on your breath … . Notice how the air enters your body and how it leaves again
- Use your vision to connect with another object – with a soft gaze consider its patterns, shapes, colours … .
- Be gentle with yourself, repeat this a few times until you are more able to hold the duality of visual cues and respiratory movements as one
- Take a couple of deeper resourcing breaths before continuing with the reflective prompts

Reference

Turgenev, I. (2017) *Fathers and Sons*. Translated by Constance Garnett, first published in 1917. U.S: Enhanced Media.

1 BLOBS

Time to Allow	Topics This Could Be Specifically Useful For
Preparation time: 2 minutes (to access images)	Reflecting on group dynamics
Reflection time: 15 minutes or more	Reflecting on our own identity and which parts of our sub-personalities were active or inactive

Why this prompt appealed to me

While I don't recall who introduced me to "blob trees" I do remember I was an immediate fan. The blob tree is the first of 50 blob scenarios drawn by Ian Long and Pip Wilson. The creators recognise that it is sometimes easier to understand our own reaction, when we see it mirrored in someone else. It is also easier to talk about something that represents our own feelings, than to talk directly about what we are experiencing as explained by Lawley and

Figure 4.1 Example blob scenario

From: The Big Book of Blobs, by Pip Wilson & Ian Long, Copyright © 2018 Routledge. Reproduced by permission of Taylor & Francis Group.

Tompkins (2000). The blob scenarios are creative resources in group and workshop settings and, as I discovered, a light-hearted entry point for my own reflection.

My favourite scene is "blob football," see Figure 4.1. I used it for a team coaching assignment and I still remember some of the labels they invented to talk about the blobs.

When I am curious about which of my mini-selves showed up with a client or group, blob football provides a playful energy. For example, when congratulating myself for a successful session, the blob doing a pirouette prompts me to consider "Am I being a bit of a prima donna?" … and if so, might I have missed the blob scoring the goal behind me? When I was taking a more observational role (perhaps the blob sitting on the goal crossbar), allowing things to unfold in front of me, could my clients have seen that as a grumpy lack of interest? This scenario is particularly helpful when reflecting on group sessions – I will consider each group member and wonder about which blob role they took, when and why.

A pathway for reflection

- Access the images
- Set an intention for reflection
- Leaf through the book and choose a blob setting to use
- Notice which blobs you are drawn to – why might that be?
- Notice which blobs you feel negative about– why might that be?
- As a result, which blobs have been overlooked – could that indicate a blind spot?
- Consider what questions the exercise raises for you
- Consider what meaning this exercise holds for you
- Notice your energy and act accordingly

References

Lawley, J. & Tompkins, P. (2000) *Metaphors in Mind: Transformation through Symbolic Modelling.* London: Developing Company Press.
Wilson, P and Long, I. (2008) *The Big Book of Blobs.* Abingdon: Routledge.

2 KINTSUGI MONTAGE

Time to Allow	Topics This Could Be Specifically Useful For
Preparation time: 2 minutes	Viewing difficult events from a more positive lens
Reflection Time: 5 minutes or more	Capturing complexity in a memorable way

Why this prompt appealed to me

I discovered the art of "kintsugi" (which translates to golden repair) through a social media post. Essentially, it is a Japanese tradition of mending broken ceramics by using resin infused with gold. See Figure 4.2. It is an art form that honours the life events of an object, inviting us to embrace the flawed and imperfect.

I like the concept of putting care into how we repair things, and the idea that kintsugi may create something even more beautiful than the original. For me this has parallels with how everyday

 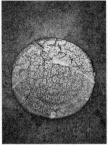 

Figure 4.2 The art of kintsugi (picture reproduced courtesy of Golden Earth Ceramics)

learning happens; we make mistakes, and they can be painful and regretful, but what we do next is critical. We can choose to see them as an opportunity for growth and leverage the mistake in a way that makes our experience fuller and more valuable than it would have been without the error occurring.

I shared this concept with a regular supervision group, creating a montage of kintsugi images. I used the montage as a departures exercise, asking which image they felt represented their learning from the session. They loved it! Now that I have the montage available, I find that it is a good aid memoire for capturing my learning. Once I have chosen an image and considered what it represents for me, I can quickly recall the details of my experience. It's like a key that unlocks a whole story book.

A pathway for reflection

* Invest some time creating a montage of kintsugi images that appeal to you
* When you have completed some client or reflective practice, peruse your montage
* Questions to ask yourself could be:

  * What parts of me have fractured?
  * How have I chosen to repair them?
  * What is the gold in my glue that helps make me stronger? More beautiful than before?
  * How prepared am I to show my broken-ness to others?

- What steps do I take to avoid becoming brittle and fragile?
- How might I bring my broken pieces together in a way that transcends my previous form?

Resources

Golden Earth Studio (2022) *Gallery*. Available at: www.thegold enearthstudio.co.uk. (Accessed: October 2022).

Goldenearth.ceramics (2022) *Traditional and modern techniques. Vintage and contemporary ceramics.* [Instagram] Undated. Available at: http://www.instagram.com/goldenearth.ceramics. (Accessed: 28 September 2022).

3 KWIRKEEZ

Acknowledgement: Paul Sanbar

Time to Allow	Topics This Could Be Specifically Useful For
Preparation time: 2 minutes Reflection time: 15 minutes or more	Clarifying which of your sub-personalities were in operation Exploring sessions where you are feeling "bent out of shape"

Why this prompt appealed to me

Kwirkeez has its foundations in the children's game "misfits" – I have articulated the exercise with clients elsewhere (Lucas, 2020). Exploring a suite of characters, each comprised of five elements (hat, head, body, right leg and left leg), you choose a variety of pieces that come together as a character which represents your current sense of self. However, noticing that the images felt dated I collaborated with Paul Sanbar to develop a new, more inclusive, set of characters. We hired a cartoonist to develop characters, and now Kwirkeez are housed on a MURAL template (see resources).

I often use Kwirkeez as an introductory exercise for a new group to help them articulate their coaching approach. I will always prepare my own so that I can role model the concept. What is interesting is that I rarely choose exactly the same pieces. I've noticed that when things are going particularly well, or conversely if I am struggling with self-care, my choices shift. See Figure 4.3 of a screenshot of two Kwirkeez.

Figure 4.3 MURAL screenshot Kwirkeez of my best self (left) and my depleted self (right)

While there's something helpful about having this exercise facilitated by another, it is also possible to play with it independently. I like to take a screenshot of my creation so that I can return to it later and notice what seems to have resolved and what might need further attention.

A pathway for reflection

- Access the Kwirkeez MURAL template via Paul Sanbar
- Create a character that represents you at your best, save this for future reference
- Bring a tricky client or work situation to mind – create a second character that represents how you were in that moment
- Place the two characters side by side – what differences are there?
- Consider which components of your best self might be helpful to you right now?
- If you were to swap these into your second character, which elements would you need to replace or let go of?
- What might this mean for what you need to do now?

Resource

Contact details for Paul Sanbar to access MURAL workshop. Available at: https://linktr.ee/pshadisanbarpcc. (Accessed: 19 September 2022).

Reference

Lucas, M. (2020) 'Misfits', in Lucas. M. (ed.) *101 Coaching Supervision Techniques, Approaches, Enquiries and Experiments.* Abingdon: Routledge, pp. 68–70.

4 LIMINAL MUSE CONVERSATION CARDS

Acknowledgement: Charlotte Housden

Time to Allow	Topics This Could Be Specifically Useful For

Preparation time:
    2 minutes (to access
    images)
	When seeking inspiration to begin reflection

Reflection time:
    15 minutes or more
	When reflecting on something and its feels
	    opaque, blocked or turgid

Why this prompt appealed to me

The images that form the Liminal Muse Conversation cards were taken by Charlotte Housden. Together we developed a series of workshops using her imagery to facilitate deeper conversations. Perhaps because I appreciate the range of Charlotte's images, and I have witnessed how they work as a projective tool, I am always curious to see what wisdom they might hold for me.

There are three editions, I mostly use Edition 1 with my own clients, so I prefer to use editions 2 and 3 for my personal reflections. They are less contaminated by memories of what other people see in the images.

I enjoy the process of perusing and choosing an image and then noticing what emerges for me. The Liminal Muse cards are now a "go to" when I am procrastinating or feel a bit stuck. Having engaged visually, it seems easier to notice where the grit is, which deserves further exploration. With this as a focus, I then use the other images in the pack to deepen my reflections further (Figure 4.4).

A pathway for reflection

- Access the images
- Set an intention for reflection
- Leaf through the cards one by one – noticing which images you are drawn to, and placing them aside
- Notice when you want to stop – sometimes when you reach the end of the pack and sometimes when a particular image feels like "enough"
- Look at the selected cards, consider what story they hold

Figure 4.4 Example liminal muse image

- Notice if it helps you form a question for further reflection or action
- Turn the cards over (they are double-sided) does this help you answer your question? Could one of the previously discarded cards offer any clues?
- Notice your energy, and act accordingly

Resources

Digital versions hosted on Deckhive. Available at: www.deckhive. com. (Accessed: 19 September 2022).
Physical decks of Liminal Muse Conversation Cards. Available at: http://liminalmuse.co.uk. (Accessed: 19 September 2022).

Reference

Housden and Lucas (2021) *Liminal Muse Goes Digital.* Toolbox: Tried and Tested. May/June, Vol 16, 3, pp. 60–61. Coaching at Work.

5 METAPHORICAL DRAWING

Time to Allow	Topics This Could Be Specifically Useful For
Preparation time: 2 minutes Reflection time: 15 minutes or more	Being curious as to what might lie outside of your awareness Being open to the question of what might need more attention

Why this prompt appealed to me

This approach helps to de-clutter my thoughts and sharpens my sense of the relational dynamics of which I am part. The idea is that a metaphor is used as a landscape in which to imagine yourself and your client, which may in turn surface some latent information. The exercise can be done in your imagination, or it can be done quite literally by drawing the scene on paper. I like the metaphor of a Desert Island and this version was included in Lucas (2020). However, many alternatives could spark your imagination – for example, the idea of a performance on stage, engaging in a sport, or working on a farm, or walking in a particular landscape. This isn't an art competition and so ironically those who are good at drawing might be distracted by perfecting their picture, better to use stick people, sketching quickly to move your reflections on.

I like this activity because by transporting myself and my client to a different place, I have to think more conceptually about what is happening in our working relationship. It's particularly useful when there is an organisational context, which is so complex I can feel overwhelmed by the detail.

A pathway for reflection

- The task is simply to choose a landscape and then start to draw (or imagine)

- A good question to get you started might be "How are you spending your time here?" You could consider where each of you are located, what you are doing, and perhaps who else knows you are here
- If you are enjoying the process, you can set yourself some more exploratory questions like:

  - How did we get here?
  - What resources are here?
  - What obstacles do we need to overcome?
  - If your client completed this activity, how similar or different would their metaphorical landscape be?
  - When will we know it's time to leave?
  - How will we leave? Together? Separately?
  - If I stay, who will I become?

Reference

Lucas, M. and Champion, C. K. (2020) 'Desert Island Fantasy', in Lucas, M. (ed.) *101 Coaching Supervision Techniques, Approaches, Enquiries and Experiments*. Abingdon: Routledge, pp. 226–228.

6 MURMURATIONS

Time to Allow	Topics This Could Be Specifically Useful For
Preparation time: 2 minutes (to access videos)	Being curious as to what might lie outside of your awareness
Reflection time: 15 minutes or more	Being open to questioning what might need more attention

Why this prompt appealed to me

As a dog walker, I have a few favourite routes – one is along the Esplanade here in Weymouth. In the spring there is a row of houses that have become a spot for flocks of starlings to roost. I hold a hope that one day I will see them take off and they'll create a murmuration just for me. It's one of those natural wonders that feels marvellous.

When planning my Reflective Practice Space sessions, a murmuration was an obvious visual prompt. There are many available on the internet – some purely visual, some accompanied by music. I have a particular favourite (see resources) and searching for the one that feels right for you, at a moment in time is an interesting exercise in itself. When I set out with an intention to reflect on my practice, using my favourite clip, different things stand out to me on each occasion. I have come to trust that this offers insight as to what I need to pay attention to.

For example, I was reflecting on a client who lacked focus and I noticed how irritated I became by the murmuration changing direction unpredictably …. But if I stuck with it, I noticed the wider shaping of the murmuration …. So how could I take a wider view with my client? Another time I was reflecting with a group in mind and noticed one of the starlings going off on its own before returning to the flock. I wondered whose attention had been diverted in the last session. I replayed some moments from the session, searching for a change in the group's energy. Nothing occurred to me. I then realised there was a moment when I had been distracted, I'd not noticed until now, the video prompted that in my awareness.

A pathway for reflection

- What kind of natural wonders might provide an interesting prompt for your reflection?
- Use the internet to create a short list of possible videos you could utilise
- Set an intention to reflect on your practice
- Watch the video and see what emerges in your awareness
- As far as possible stick with those moments where you notice resistance or irritation arising …. What happens then …?
- Consider what learning is emerging and what you are motivated to do next

Resource

Keep turning left (2010) *Amazing starlings murmuration (full HD)*. Available at: https://www.youtube.com/watch?v=eakKfY5aHmY. (Accessed: 1 August 2022).

7 OPTICAL ILLUSIONS

Time to Allow	Topics This Could Be Specifically Useful For
Preparation time: 2 minutes (to access images) Reflection time: 15 minutes or more	When feeling blinkered or wondering if your responses are a bit siloed or habituated When you lack curiosity about a client, situation or context

Why this prompt appealed to me

This prompt evolved from a presentation about group supervision, where I used the optical illusion entitled "Forever Always" by the living artist, Octavio Ocampo, to illustrate how together we can see more. The exercise helped draw attention to our habits in how we look at things, which in turn influences our thoughts and perspectives:

• Whatever shapes we see first, we tend to see first next time
• When we are told there are other items in the picture and we apply conscious effort, we can see them as well (for some this requires more guidance than others)
• As we open our minds to the possibility that the image holds more, our curiosity increases and we start to actively look for new elements
• We can deliberately shift our eyes and in doing so shift our perspective; in turn that enables new items to come into our awareness (see an example in Figure 4.5)
• When we reflect with others, they will see different elements at different times and hold different interpretations of what the illusion shows Figure 4.5

When my energy for reflection is low, I recognise this may be because I am operating in a blind spot or bringing assumptions and habits into my practice. The original illusion reminds me of what more a situation probably holds. Searching for a new optical illusion seems to re-enliven my curiosity and invites me to test myself. As a result, my complacent energy fades and I can transfer my more curious energy to my reflections.

Figure 4.5 Example optical illusion

A pathway for reflection

- Access an optical illusion
- Notice your gut reaction – what biases might that indicate in your thinking about your current practice?
- Attempt to understand more about the image – which sense did you apply? Logic, emotion, imagination? What senses are you applying when with your clients?
- What other interpretations could there be for this image? How could you interpret your practice differently?

- Ask yourself what might other people see that you have yet to see? Apply this same question to your work?
- Consider when enough is enough and/or find another optical illusion and repeat the process

Resources

Illusions.org (2022) *A selection of the most populist & cool optical illusions*. Available at: www.illusions.org. (Accessed: 5 July 2022).

Optical illusions portal (no date). Available at: www.opticalillusions portal.com. (Accessed: 5 July 2022).

The work of Octavio Ocampo can be viewed on: Visions Fine Art's website: https://www.visionsfineart.com/ocampo/index.html. Visions Fine Art is the Agent, Representative, Publisher for Octavio Ocampo, all rights reserved.

Wikiart (no date). *Octavio Ocampo*. Available at: http://www. wikiart.org/en/octavio-ocampo. (Accessed: 19 July 2022).

8 RETHINK.LY BY DAVID TINKER

Time to Allow	Topics This Could Be Specifically Useful For
15 minutes to follow the "relationship problem" process	Reviewing a client relationship to deepen empathy and insight

Why this approach appealed to me

I've had a love of psychodrama and sociodrama ever since seeing it live on TV as a teenager. There was something magic about enacting someone's thoughts and feelings visually and bringing to life the "unspoken" and "unseen" in relationships. The part of me that was interested in understanding more deeply about the human condition was inspired. Since then, this approach has informed my coaching and supervision practise, and regularly enabled insights for myself and for clients.

The Rethink.ly digital tool uses avatars in a 3D world to create a dynamic visual representation of relationships and situations, see Figure 4.6. The ProReal "engine" at the heart of the tool has been

Figure 4.6 Screenshot of Rethink.ly illustrating internal narrative of the user

used in the NHS to support mental health, and commercial organisations to support online coaching. Since its launch in 2015, useful
evidence has been gathered about ProReal's ability to generate new
insights and to increase levels of self-awareness.

The software design is based on Moreno's concepts of "socio-
metry" and "role reversal" to enable users to visually describe relationships, and then "step into the shoes" of others. This helps
to increase empathy and encourages the user to take different perspectives. The visual representation can then be sent to others so
they can share in the new perspective, perhaps as a prompt for
additional dialogue.

As a supervision tool this software offers a quick self-help review
of a client situation. Its automated prompts guide the user through a
simple reflection process with options to deepen awareness or explore alternatives for how to move the relationship forward.

A pathway for reflection

- Set an intention to reflect upon your client work
- Access Rethink.ly through the QR code below
- Follow the prompts on the screen
- You may choose to share the visual representation with a
  colleague or supervisor

Resources

Please use this QR code to go directly to Rethink.ly

ProReal (undated) *Press the pause button and focus on your wellbeing.*
Available at: www.think.ly. (Accessed: 1 October 2022).

Further reading

Moreno, J. L. (1987) *The Essential Moreno: Writings on Psychodrama, Group Method, and Spontaneity.* US: Springer Publishing Company.
Sternberg, P. and Garcia, A. (2000) *Sociodrama: Who's in Your Shoes?* Connecticut: Greenwood Publishing Group.

9 SELF-REFLECTIVE SHAPES BY HANNAH BUTLER

Time to Allow	Topics This Could Be Specifically Useful For
Preparation time: 2 minutes	Capturing how your reflections are unfolding, knowing that some insights are with you and deserve further inspection
Reflection time: 15 minutes or more	Creating an aide memoire that you want to return to

Why this prompt appealed to me

I find that the visual manipulation of images has a profound effect on my thinking. The science would say that this is because the process activates areas within the brain (frontal lobe, temporal lobe, cerebellum, occipital lobe, parietal lobe) and our imagination stimulates broad networks of the brain areas to work together harmoniously, leading to cerebral benefits.

This approach was developed by Kirkman and Brownhill (2020) who are both leading thinkers in education and learning. Their approach which involves selecting and drawing shapes while developing questions for reflection, offers the opportunity to express and balance both explicit and tacit knowledge. Integrating shapes, words and images when working with ill-defined matters creates a stimulating context, which encourages us to generate our own perspectives. The very process of drawing a particular shape and of there being no rules around where the text need be located helps to disrupt the more traditional use of prose or narrative. Importantly the shape emulates containment thereby fostering more disruption within a place of safety.

I routinely create a self-reflective shape after my own supervision, Figure 4.7 is one example. I add the colours after the initial reflection as this enables me to consider how a colour is representative of an emotion for me. This enables me to fully view the emotional and cognitive landscape of my reflection and practice.

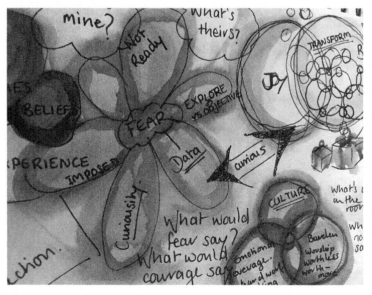

Figure 4.7 Example self-reflective shape post supervision (reproduced with permission from Hannah Butler)

A pathway for reflection

- Draw any 2D shape on paper or device. This can be a regular or abstract shape, you can decide. The shape may have significance to you, or it can have no particular meaning
- Once you have an outline shape you can then add in segments, if you haven't already done so. The lines you use for division can be faint or hard, thick or thin, wavy or straight, dotted or joined
- Identify questions you would like to answer. You can use questions from a model in the literature or develop your own
- Once the questions are set, decide on the subject of your reflection, perhaps a relationship, a coaching session, a body of work, an itch you can't quite scratch …
- Start to add your responses to the different segments, feel free to use colour and get creative

Reference

Kirkman, P. and Brownhill, S. (2020) 'Refining Professional Knowing as a Creative Practice: Towards a Framework for Self-Reflective Shapes and a Novel Approach to Reflection', *Reflective Practice: International and Multidisciplinary Perspectives*, 21(1), pp. 94–109.

10 THE BOY AND THE BUTTERFLY

Time to Allow	Topics This Could Be Specifically Useful For
Preparation time: 2 minutes to access the video	Considering how you manage your tendency to rescue, or not
Reflection time: 15 minutes or more	Being open to the possibility that, however unintentionally, you may have caused harm to another

Why this approach appealed to me

I first saw a version of this fable as a video clip at a coaching conference. I thought the message was an inspired choice because as helping practitioners we often need to manage our desire to rescue.

I have only watched the video once, that was enough. The impact of the story was so strong it has stayed with me. When I am with a client and I feel my own urge to rescue arise in me, it is almost immediately accompanied by an image of a pair of scissors and the chrysalis (this will make sense once you see the video). Similarly, when I notice my client struggle, to articulate a thought, to engage in an experiment which I have my doubts about – I remember the necessity of the butterfly to pump blood into its new wings. I am more able to be with them in their struggle, recognising how easy it would be for me to "help" and in doing so cause more harm than good.

A pathway for reflection

- Access the video suggested in the resources, or one that is similar
- What does the fable evoke in you?
- What do you know about your own desires to help and rescue?
- What is your tipping point at which you get out your metaphorical scissors, in an attempt to liberate something for your client?
- How are you when your client seems exhausted with their struggle?
- When might you have acted with good intention, only to find you have caused harm?

Resource

Winspire Magazine (2017). *The boy and the butterfly – an inspirational story about life*. Available at: https://youtu.be/4majrQ6pOuY. (Accessed: 24 August 2022).

11 THREE LITTLE BIRDS

Time to Allow	Topics This Could Be Specifically Useful For
Preparation time: 2 minutes (to access video) Reflection time: 5 minutes or more	When you are looking for random inspiration to fuel reflection

Why this prompt appealed to me

I came across this video clip while on social media, there was something about the energy in the little boy's face that almost demanded I see what it was about. My attention span online is typically short and yet having started to watch him singing, I was hooked. I watched it, again. I found myself smiling with him, and tears of joy welled in my eyes. I knew I wanted to share it with my Reflective Practice Space participants. There is just so much to marvel at ... his enjoyment, his musicality, his ability to memorise the words, his expressions. I started to wonder about his parents – what did this say about their nurturing, their encouragement, the way in which they developed and then shared his talent?

I am not sure what relevance this has for our client work, I am only sure that it feels worthy of inclusion here.

A pathway for reflection

- Access and watch the video
- Notice your responses ...

  - What emotions arise?
  - What does it make you curious about?

- What utility might this have for your personal or professional life?
- Are you pleased or irritated that it is included here?

Resource

Majically News (2020) *This precious child singing "Three Little Birds" by Bob Marley will fill you with hope & happiness.* Available at: http://https://youtu.be/q1ZRI0zVpY4. (Accessed: 24 August 2022).

12 TIMING MAP JIGSAWS

Time to Allow	Topics This Could Be Specifically Useful For
Preparation time: 2 minutes to find your session notes Reflection time: 15 minutes or more	When noticing your memory of a session is patchy and you want to ensure you have a more comprehensive sense of what occurred

Why this prompt appealed to me

I developed this approach when I noticed that reflecting upon a client session some days later, my memory was patchy. While I could often remember how the session started and ended, the middle section was often blurred. Working with my typically scant notes, I began to piece together parts of the conversation, I would add more scribbles to my page, in a mind-map fashion.

Overtime, I developed a method for checking the comprehensiveness of my memory, which I describe here. Interestingly, I rarely remember the entirety of the conversation, but through this process, I am more confident that I understand what contributed to the turning points and/or the clunks in the conversation. Where there are gaps, I consider whether this may have been because I in flow, or because I had become distracted. Being open to the latter possibility enables me to be honest with myself, and in turn, consider what may have caused the distraction.

A pathway for reflection

- Retrieve your notes from the session in question
- Map out a clock face to represent the whole of the session time – and chunk it into three sections, illustrating the time you typically allocate for the opening, middle and close of the dialogue
- Transfer your notes onto the clock face – what do you notice about where they fit?
- Replay the session in your mind's eye, and place any additional jottings in the appropriate segment of the clock face

- How comprehensive is your record?
- Do any gaps bother you?
- What is your sense of what was happening in those moments when you have no notes or memory?
- Where there are distractions that relate more to you than to your client – what personal work is asking for your attention?

Anecdotes from practitioners using visual prompts

Three little birds

What shifted as a result of the exercise?

Me letting go of fear. I responded emotionally and connected. I agreed with the song and believed in the song. It encouraged me to be open.

How did you feel about the experience?

Child shaking its head, beautiful connection through his eyes. Open, really seeing. Such re-assurance, it appealed to the child in me – almost as if the child was singing to younger child and that younger child was me. As I let go of fear, I am more creative and more open. Interestingly quite a visceral experience again as I am recalling the experience to write this.

RPS Participant, January 2022

Blobs (river)

What shifted as a result of the exercise?

The Blobs represent lots of little pieces of work and a few big chunks. I wanted to simplify and be more present to me. I was tired, and my attention during the mindfulness check-in wandered. I spotted negatives in the blob expressions and postures and had to look hard for positives. The solid structure strengthened my need to firm up my transition from full-time working to retirement.

What did I want for this journey? The river and different trees highlighted appreciation for nature and people important to me.

How did you feel about the reflective experience?

Maybe because of my low energy or the busy-ness of the picture I "fought" my way to making this technique useful. Others shared they used more than one technique whereas I'd started so I was going to finish. My life is pretty good for most of the time and yet I don't acknowledge it to me – interesting!

RPS Participant, February 2021

5

AUDITORY PROMPTS TO
AID REFLECTION

AN INTRODUCTION TO REFLECTING WITH AUDITORY PROMPTS

Many of us will use music as "background noise" – perhaps it will fill the space as you drive, perhaps it will influence your pace when you exercise or when you do household chores. If you play an instrument, perhaps you will use it to help express how you feel in the moment.

In this section, you may choose to use auditory cues to mask unwanted background noise and to create an appropriate ambience for reflection. You may also use them as prompts in their own right. For example, you might listen to the tracks provided to see what is evoked in you and then turn to the reflective prompts provided to expand your awareness. Over time you may find it possible to do both concurrently.

As you experience each of the auditory prompts which follow, do so where you can, with a beginner's ear. Rather than considering whether you enjoy the piece or not, focus on the sounds from a more observational perspective. Three types of auditory prompts are provided:

Musical

For these prompts place your attention on what instruments you can identify, consider the musicality of the piece – the rhythm, the beat, the sense of harmony or discord. When you are able to take a less personal perspective on a piece, then we encourage you to notice

DOI: 10.4324/9781003311188-6

what other sensations it evokes in you. Perhaps it will trigger emotions, memories or possibilities … any of which could be useful when you reflect on your client practice.

Soundscapes

The coaching community is embracing research like that of Mind (2022) which suggests that natural environments can benefit mental and physical wellbeing. There is recognition that "blue and green" spaces have a restorative power. We have built on this idea with our locational and weather soundscapes. While we may not have immediate and safe access to the natural environment, we offer here auditory prompts that attempt to emulate them. This carefully curated set of soundscapes can help transport our minds deep into the natural world, from the comfort of our usual workspace. The soundscapes may evoke memories of where you met that sound before. While honouring that memory – move beyond the content such that you can notice what emotions and sensations come along with it in the present. The reflective prompts which accompany these soundscapes were designed with your client in mind, however, you might also adapt them by asking the same questions of yourself.

Soundbaths and binaural beats

These prompts may seem unusual at first. We invite you to start the experiment and notice your response. Of course, if something feels odd, this may detract your energy from your reflections. However, it could be that overcoming resistance to difference is useful when attempted in service of your clients. Therefore, rather than abandoning the prompt forever, find a time when you can re-visit it and be curious about how you experience it the second time around.

In compiling this section, I discovered the work of Dr. Stéphane Pigeon and his website myNoise. What he offers is quite unique, the opportunity to create your own soundscape, leveraging recordings of real sounds gathered over many years. To simplify the process of creating your own auditory experience, we offer links to take you to the different libraries of sounds. Alternatively, each template provides suggested tracks from i-tunes, Spotify (we offer a QR Code, so you may need a QR Code reader) and YouTube.

Participants of the Reflective Practice Space sessions suggest selecting or creating your soundscape separately from the reflective space, as it becomes a voyage of discovery in and of itself and will eat into your protected time.

A mindfulness exercise to help you prepare for reflecting with auditory prompts

- Find a space where you will be uninterrupted
- Bring your attention to your breath
- Notice how the air enters your body and how it leaves again
- Place your attention to your ears – what sounds are you aware of
- You may find it helpful to close your eyes or to lower your gaze ... take another in-breath and another out-breath .... What can you hear now?
- Move your attention to the sounds in the room you are in – perhaps a clock ticking, or a printer humming
- On an in-breath, welcome in those sounds you are aware of
- On an out-breath, release the sounds in your awareness in readiness for whatever comes next
- Move your attention inwards – perhaps you can hear your arm brush your desk, your stomach gurgle or the blood pump in your ears
- On an in-breath, welcome in those sounds you are aware of
- On an out-breath, release the sounds in your awareness in readiness for whatever comes next
- Now move your attention outwards – beyond what is in the room to hear what lies beyond. Perhaps the conversations of other people nearby, traffic outside or rain against your window
- On an in-breath, welcome in those sounds you are aware of
- On an out-breath, release the sounds in your awareness in readiness for whatever comes next
- Now return your attention to the sounds in your immediate environment – what do you recognise from before? What else do you now hear?
- Gently lower the intensity of your auditory awareness while continuing to give attention to your breath. If you closed your eyes, you may find that you wish to open them now
- Take a couple of deeper resourcing breaths before continuing with the reflective prompts

Reference

Mind (2022). *Go Green to Beat the Blues*. Available at: http://www. mind.org.uk/news-campaigns/news/go-green-to-beat-the-blues/ (Accessed: 29 September 2022).

1 EXPERIMENTING WITH BINAURAL BEATS BY DR. IR. STÉPHANE PIGEON

Time to Allow	Topics This Could Be Specifically Useful for
30 minutes	When seeking to create a particular brain state in support of your reflective activities

I have recently been introduced to Dr. Ir. Stéphane Pigeon; his website myNoise allows you to create your own soundscape. Here we focus on binaural beats, before starting, you need to understand a little more about how it works.

Why this approach appeals to me

The brain is an electrochemical organ. Its electrical activity, caused by the neurons communicating with each other, can be recorded using an electroencephalogram. While the activity of a single neuron is too weak to register, the waves emanating from billions of neurons can be measured. The electrical activity is categorised according to frequency. The low Delta frequencies are associated with Sleep; the higher Alpha and Beta waves with focus and alertness.

In physics, the principle of resonance, that one object can transmit its vibration to another, is indisputable. Whether resonance can be applied between a sound and the electrochemical activity of our brain, has been the source of passionate debates. The notion of "brainwave entrainment" refers to the capacity of the brain to naturally synchronise its brainwave frequencies with the rhythm of an external stimulus; in this context, a sound. Without getting too technical, binaural beats are one way of embedding the frequency of a brainwave (too low to be heard) into an audible sound. Given the principle of resonance, purists propose using binaural beats with a frequency related to the brain state you want to achieve. To relax, they suggest Delta waves and for productivity, the higher frequencies, Alpha or

Beta. Isochronic Tones and Bilateral Modulations are two other ways to embed brainwave frequencies into audible sounds.

So ... does this really work? Even among the scientific community, there is no consensus. My recommendation is to experiment by yourself and see what happens. From my experience, the frequency of the binaural beat doesn't matter much. Simply use a setting that feels comfortable, which you can play quietly and still hear above the background noise of your room. Then frame your mind into the effect you want to achieve. You won't even hear the binaural beat after a while, because it is so steady, but it is still there.

I have used binaural beats to facilitate me writing this piece; I didn't pause, I didn't feel uninspired the time passed quickly and I don't particularly enjoy writing! Is this evidence of synchronicity working as advertised by the proponent of the brainwave entrainment technique, or is it simply the power of suggestion? Does it really matter if it is useful for you? Why not experiment and see what happens?

A pathway for reflection

- Ensure you have an appreciation of what binaural beats are and the different brain states they can create
- Set a frame for your reflection, perhaps you want to stop procrastinating, perhaps you want to re-charge after a challenging session or to ignite your thinking following a period of boredom
- Play with the possibilities provided by myNoise to create your own soundscape
- Use the soundscape created to accompany you, the binaural beat playing in the background will remind your unconscious mind of the frame you set

Resources

Pigeon, S. (2012–2022) *Binaural Beat Machine*. Available at: http://myNoi.se/BINAURAL (Accessed: 26 September 2022).

Pigeon, S. (2012–2022) *Isochronic Tones*. Available at: http://myNoi.se/ISOCHRONIC (Accessed: 26 September 2022).

Pigeon, S. (2012–2022) *Bilateral Harmonics*. Available at: http://myNoi.se/BILATERAL (Accessed: 26 September 2022).

2 CREATE YOUR OWN PLAYLIST BY CLAIRE KITAY

Time to Allow	Additional Resources or Preparation Required	Topics This Could Be Specifically Useful for
Preparation time: 30–60 minutes	Access to Spotify Earphones or headphones	When a flexible range of stimuli are needed to aid reflection

Many of us are familiar with the idea of using a playlist – maybe for exercise or long distance journeys. When we use one in these situations, we are using the music to maintain our energy, pass the time, block out sounds that distract or annoy and/or simply relax and switch off.

To use a playlist in a more focused manner, we need to think clearly about the purpose of the music chosen. Rather than being directly for our personal enjoyment, it is the emotions that are brought to the surface by the music, rather than the music itself, that are relevant here. It may be that a track creates for *you* a feeling of sadness, irritation, joy and calm (as some examples). Remember that this is your subjective response and may not be shared by another listener – in other words, it is not the music itself, but the listener's response that is important.

In exploring and choosing music for a playlist, try to avoid songs with lyrics. Lyrics often conflict with the music itself – many are about rejection, social and contemporary issues and relationships. Lyrics force an atmosphere that may not be generated by the accompanying music.

A pathway for reflection

- Considering the emotional aspects of your practice, think about whether creating your own playlist could help identify, and reflect upon themes within your practice
- Using your preferred music streaming service, choose some search terms to find atmospheric music that might create an emotional reaction in you, and then explore some of the suggestions. For example:

- Concepts like landscapes, nature or wild nature
- Geographical search terms such as Mediterranean, Caribbean, desert and forest

- Look for tracks between two and four minutes ideally – this is about optimum for a listening exercise. Long enough to get absorbed by the music and short enough not to become distracted and switch off
- Review the choices you have made, considering the variety and purpose of the tracks in your playlist: Calming, energising and picking up difficult emotions such as anger and help-lessness. What might be needed to ensure you have created a balanced list?

Resources

Here is a sample list of my own – this may open up some ideas for you.

Please use this QR code to go directly to the playlist.

Kitay, C. M. (2022) *Sample Playlist*. Available at: https://open. spotify.com/playlist/4BYDEkqDVEmKhS2alwpy0L?si=a76ee28 bfd1341f1 (Accessed: 26 September 2022).

List of music as presented in Spotify playlist:

Hawgood, I. (2021) 'Fractural', 朝. Available at: https://open. spotify.com/track/0vIk5Z6dAqWeOQoE76NUTv?si=7a0be4fd 7e1e4a76 (Accessed: 26 September 2022).

Chuck Plaisance and Suzanne Doucet (1998) 'Zen Garden', *Tranquility*. Available at: https://open.spotify.com/track/4rn2BnxLvxIobCLUE 96y1R?si=78b06edf97cc44f5 (Accessed: 26 September 2022).

Fanfara Tirana (2013) 'Mediterrane #1', *Rough Guide to the Mediterranean*. Available at: https://open.spotify.com/track/1afdWtTSWS6Aeqj 24oaZOG?si=5ef7669df4c94758 (Accessed: 26 September 2022).

Abdhulla Ibrahim (2000) 'Soweto', *Cape Town Revisited*. Available at: https://open.spotify.com/track/7ocJaxAVByjmdZ3L37npC 5?si=ae456fdd24ef46a8 (Accessed: 26 September 2022).

London Mozart Players (1995) 'Piano Concerto No.21 in C Major, K.467; II. Andante, *Mozart: Piano Concertos, Vol. 6*. Available at: https://open.spotify.com/track/429GaRIWKJ3EU1GAQPb Lcr?si=4d5b20c67b5845df (Accessed: 26 September 2022).

Sheku Kanneh-Mason (2018) 'Hallelujah (arr. Hodge)', *Inspiration*. Available at: https://open.spotify.com/track/7q2DehTTvivpur Qfe41iCy?si=0a897cb407744af8 (Accessed: 26 September 2022).

3 LOCATION SOUNDSCAPE: CITYSCAPE BY MARGARET MACAFEE

Time to Allow	Topics This Could Be Specifically Useful for
Preparation time: 2 minutes Reflection time: Set a timer	When a client needs to embrace experimentation, discover new energy or possibilities

For me, the urban soundscape is about identity, context and possibilities. The identities we adopt in our everyday lives are likely to have some sort of stability and familiarity. They are very much shaped by the contexts in which we typically find ourselves and the characters we encounter. Travelling to a new town or city, for work or holiday, gives us the perfect opportunity to accentuate aspects of our core identity or try out different identities for a short period of time with people who have no prior reference point for us. We can experiment with a new language and climate-appropriate clothing, while embracing local customs and cuisine. What shifts when we adopt a "beginner's mind" to our self-expression or the adoption of new habits? How can we take this more experimental side of our-selves back to re-energise the everyday? I find this approach parti-cularly helpful in situations when a client might be feeling stuck or dissatisfied with routine. Referencing such gentle experimentation can often encourage the deeper changes necessary to move them forward.

A pathway to reflection

- Set an intention to reflect upon your clients
- Select a track from the resources provided (or create your own), set a timer (for long tracks) or set the repeat loop (for short tracks) to boundary your reflective space
- Consider the reflective prompts as follows

Reflective prompts

- Imagine your client has taken a holiday. Choose the soundscape that you think best reflects a preferred location or, alternatively, somewhere which would feel uncomfortable
- If a vibrant metropolitan or urban soundscape has been chosen – think about what needs this city is satisfying for your client? Is it excitement, adventure, "the buzz," escapism or perhaps a stark contrast to their current circumstances?
- If a charming village has been chosen – think about what your client is looking for in this gentle setting, far from the crowds. Perhaps an immersion into the community, revelling in historic architecture, embracing the opportunity to explore on foot and adopt a slower pace of life, to venture into countryside from a welcoming local base?
- What learning is there from this different pace and scale of life that could be taken back to the current reality? Where can inspiration or "recharging" opportunities be found? By contrast, what might drain energy away?
- What risks can be taken and under what circumstances? Might there be a need to linger for a while in safe territory?
- To close: What is in your awareness now? What feels complete? What needs more attention?

Resources

- Create your own City Soundscape using myNoise.net.
- http://myNoi.se/PARIS (Accessed: 22 August 2022).
- http://mynoi.se/MEXICOCITY (Accessed: 22 August 2022).
- http://mynoi.se/SENEGAL (Accessed: 22 August 2022).

Alternatively, access one or more of these suggested tracks:

Audio References	
iTunes	Jocelyn Robert (2011) '*The Madness of Omkareshwar*', Soundscapes - Listen to Nature. (Version 1.14, 2022). Available at: https://apps.apple.com/app/id1470589737 (Accessed: 15 June 2022).
	Jim Metzner (2017) '*Noon Bells, St Peter's Abbey*', Soundscapes - Listen to Nature. (Version 1.14, 2022). Available at: https://apps.apple.com/app/id1470589737 (Accessed: 30 July 2022).
	Jocelyn Robert (2011) '*Evening Prayer at Amarkantak*', Soundscapes - Listen to Nature. (Version 1.14, 2022). Available at: https://apps.apple.com/app/id1470589737 (Accessed: 25 September 2022).
	Rain Rain Sleep Sounds. (Version 6.9.3, 2022) *Harbour Seagulls*. [download] Available at: https://apps.apple.com/gb/app/rain-rain-sleep-sounds/id478687481 (Accessed: 25 September 2022).
Spotify	Sound Ideas (2014) *Marrakech, Morocco Lively Square Ambience With Heavy Crowd Walla & Horse Walking Past.* [download] Available at: https://open.spotify.com/track/7CpyKmvxTpVscHSFbQOgQM?si=d0ebfc357ad74849 (Accessed: 25 September 2022).
	Sound Ideas (2014) *Paris, France Restaurant Ambience With a Large Crowd & Busy Voices & Dish Noises.* [download] Available at: https://open.spotify.com/track/2JCisE5HD0O0JPbmLKfy4r?si=634a8e7f106746b5 (Accessed: 25 September 2022).
	Sound Ideas (2014) *Brazilian Market Scene With Lots of Sellers and Activity.* [download] Available at: https://open.spotify.com/track/7MKJFp0xPaYqwarCe9MKts?si=6467e16a086b4df7 (Accessed: 25 September 2022).

Audio References	
YouTube	Sound Ideas (2014) *Japan: Outdoor Playground or Park Ambience With Children Playing.* [download] Available at: https://open.spotify.com/track/2gAVR5YrX6EHAg5jRQOEBX?si=55e6bb46e1cb42ca (Accessed: 25 September 2022). Nomadic Ambience (28 March 2019) *New York City Ambience Sounds	10 Hours (City Sounds, Traffic, Sound Effects, Times Square) 4k.* [download] Available at: https://www.youtube.com/watch?v=YF3pj_3mdMc (Accessed: 25 September 2022). 4K Urban Life (10 March 2020) *4K Amsterdam, Netherlands - Urban Relax Video With City Sounds.* [download] Available at: https://www.youtube.com/watch?v=FnL2g5l8JgY (Accessed: 25 September 2022). Autumn Cozy (7 March 2021) *COZY ITALIAN VILLAGE AMBIENCE: Relaxing Nature Sounds, Fountain Sounds, Horse Cabs, Bell Sounds.* [download] Available at: https://www.youtube.com/watch?v=dqfYMPd0bgM (Accessed: 15 June 2022). Relax With Nature (13 March 2015) *Sounds of Paris.* [download] Available at: https://www.youtube.com/watch?v=kw3beC2xQgo (Accessed: 15 June 2022).

4 LOCATION SOUNDSCAPE: FOREST BY MARGARET MACAFEE

Time to Allow	Topics This Could Be Specifically Useful for
Preparation time: 2 minutes Reflection time: Set a timer	When a client is navigating a complex set of relationships to access support, receive recognition or make a wider impact

The forest soundscape helps us to deepen our understanding of the complex ecosystems in which we all thrive. The trees, plants and animals found within the forest co-exist in delicate balance with each other, from canopy to forest floor. They are constantly adapting to changes in soil, climate and human intervention. Like the forest inhabitants, our survival depends on the many symbiotic relationships we have within our associated communities. There are often complex conventions as to how we cooperate and compete for desired resources or outcomes. Our experience and profile within different groups may vary enormously. The most fulfilling are sources of kinship, connection and enrichment. Conversely, we may exist on the fringes of others, striving to make ourselves visible and our voices heard. With this expansive context in mind, we are invited to consider the voices within our ecosystems and the nature of the ensuing chorus. Thinking about prominent voices and their frequency can be revelatory.

A pathway for reflection

- Set an intention to reflect upon your clients
- Select a track from the resources provided (or create your own), set a timer (for long tracks) or set the repeat loop (for short tracks) to boundary your reflective space
- Consider the provided reflective prompts as follows

Reflective prompts

- Fixate on one sound from the forest as the voice of your client …
- Notice the surrounding chorus of sounds and voices. Which sound or whose voice dominates? How do others react to the rhythm they create?
- Consider how this environment relates to your client's setting … What other information comes to mind? Is it peaceful, energetic or frenetic even? Is it melodic or discordant? Would it be helpful for some voices or sounds to be muted or to gently disappear altogether?
- Do you sense multiple conversations happening concurrently? Is everyone listening carefully before responding or merely waiting for the chance to speak?
- Consider the sources of conflict/tension/anxiety within their relationships
- Consider where peace/harmony/resourcefulness could emanate from

- Reflect on the unexpected sounds that suddenly appear, without fanfare. Is there anticipation or preparedness on the part of your client?
- To close: What is in your awareness now? What feels complete? What needs more attention?

Resources

Create your own Forest Soundscape using MyNoise.net.
Available at: http://myNoi.se/FOREST (Accessed: 22 August 2022).
Available at: http://myNoi.se/FOREST2 (Accessed: 22 August 2022).
Available at: http://myNoi.se/FOREST3 (Accessed: 22 August 2022).

Alternatively, access one or more of these suggested tracks:

Audio References	
iTunes	Félix Blume (2017) *'Toucans in the Amazon Rainforest'*, Soundscapes - Listen to Nature. (Version 1.14, 2022). Available at: https://apps.apple.com/app/id1470589737 (Accessed: 30 July 2022).
	Frédéric Nogray (No date assigned) *'Canal con Bujajas'*, Soundscapes - Listen to Nature. (Version 1.14, 2022). Available at: https://apps.apple.com/app/id1470589737 (Accessed: 30 July 2022).
	Yannick Dauby (2013–2016) *'Taipingshan'*, Soundscapes - Listen to Nature. (Version 1.14, 2022). Available at: https://apps.apple.com/app/id1470589737 (Accessed: 30 July 2022).
	Nature Soundscapes. (Version 1.7, 2020) *WILDERNESS – Woods*. [download] Available at: https://apps.apple.com/gb/app/nature-soundscapes/id971949061 (Accessed: 01 August 2022).
Spotify	Nature Soundscape (2015) *Daytime Jungle Ambience With Heavy Insects, Birds and Water Dropping on Vegetation*. [download] Available at: https://open.spotify.com/track/4JflIJr0YVezLxTpHK5Nz3?si=1fd49d1f1cfb48d3 (Accessed: 01 August 2022).

(*Continued*)

Audio References	
	Forest Soundscapes (2015) *Afternoon Bird Chorus*. [download] Available at: https://open.spotify.com/track/0rxCggh 9HxS2NVDqKuioPu?si=109157ab28aa4b5c (Accessed: 23 September 2022).
	Wildtones Nature Sounds (2018) *The Forest at Night: Frogs and Distant Barred Owl Calls*. [download] Available at: https://open.spotify.com/track/6TNK8ROAnCa8OYC 8hgpFRe?si=4548cefed3c440dc (Accessed: 23 September 2022).
	Forest Sounds (2017) *Forest Sounds*. [download] Available at: https://open.spotify.com/track/49vFr1gfxI02psYbHuWu 6c?si=bc9e6342102d4b13 (Accessed: 23 September 2022).
YouTube	Music of Nature (10 May 2021) *Beautiful Spring Mountain Forest. Birdsong in the Caucasus Forest*. [download] Available at: https://www.youtube.com/watch?v=M0AWBnAv 8VE (Accessed: 30 July 2022).
	The Guild of Ambience (6 April 2017) *Forest Sounds	Woodland Ambience, Bird Song*. [download] Available at: https://www.youtube.com/watch?v=xNN7iTA57jM (Accessed: 30 July 2022).
	The Silent Watcher (25 September 2017) *4K Forest Birdsong 2 - Birds Sing in the Woods - No Loop Realtime Birdsong - Relaxing Nature Video*. [download] Available at: https://www.youtube.com/watch?v=XxP8kxUn5bc (Accessed: 3 August 2022).

5 LOCATION SOUNDSCAPE: MOUNTAINS BY MARGARET MACAFEE

Time to Allow	Topics This Could Be Specifically Useful for
Preparation time: 2 minutes Reflection time: Set a timer	When a client is facing a sizeable challenge that requires courage, determination and a degree of pragmatism

A hike in the mountains offers me an abundance of opportunities to take stock of life. The physicality of an upward climb is symbolic of the effort-reward cycle associated with significant, valued milestones. The panoramic view at the summit can deliver a clarity that was absent in the foothills. The journey to the summit or the descent to "basecamp" might prompt a realisation that one has underestimated the task at hand. Amidst the discomfort and apprehension lie important learning opportunities. Our success may be contingent on others, to whom we owe our best effort. The choice of and interaction with companions can also be informative. We may be called upon to take roles outside of what is comfortable – to navigate, to bolster morale or to hold back and let others lead. The mountains evoke a contemplation on our readiness to seek out audacious challenges, our flexibility and preparedness. There are opportunities for growth, regardless of outcome.

A pathway for reflection

- Set an intention to reflect upon your clients
- Select a track from the resources provided (or create your own), set a timer (for long tracks) or set the repeat loop (for short tracks) to boundary your reflective space
- Consider the reflective prompts provided

Reflective prompts

- Imagine you are walking in the mountain range with your client on a bright clear day …
- Reflect on the conversation you have had. Where are you in your journey upwards to the peak?
- Does your client have an instinctive sense of their own navigation through this place?
- How are they harnessing their energy(ies) to reach the summit?
- Do they have the stamina to sustain the pace, even when the ground is slippery, rocky or tricky underfoot? What if the wind picks up or the rain begins to fall?
- Have they brought all the necessary equipment with them for the journey? Are they overburdened with items they simply do not need?

- Focus, if you can, on the stream as it flows steadily down the mountain …
- Consider the gravitational force that transports water from the peak down into the valley below. Is your client following the flow or are they swimming upstream, against the tide?
- Is your client stopping to take in the landscape at regular intervals? What prompts them to pause? What spurs them to carry on? Would they know if they need to correct their course?
- To close: What is in your awareness now? What feels complete? What needs more attention?

Resources

Create your own Mountain Soundscape using myNoise.net.
Available at: http://myNoi.se/CANTAL (Accessed: 22 August 2022).
Available at: http://myNoi.se/GRASSLAND (Accessed: 22 August 2022).
Available at: http://myNoi.se/TIERRADEFUEGO (Accessed: 22 August 2022).

Alternatively, access one or more of these suggested tracks:

Audio References	
iTunes	Elliot Lang (2017) '*Cascades Watersong*', Soundscapes - Listen to Nature. (Version 1.14, 2022). Available at: https://apps.apple.com/app/id1470589737 (Accessed: 30 July 2022). Jocelyn Robert (2005) '*Telluic Pyrenees*', Soundscapes - Listen to Nature. (Version 1.14, 2022). Available at: https://apps.apple.com/app/id1470589737 (Accessed: 30 July 2022). Jeanne Debarsy (No date assigned).'*During That Time in the Carpathians*', Soundscapes - Listen to Nature. (Version 1.14, 2022). [download] Available at: https://apps.apple.com/app/id1470589737 (Accessed: 30 July 2022). Nature Soundscapes. (Version 1.7, 2020) *STREAM – Cool Renewal*. [download] Available at: https://apps.apple.com/gb/app/nature-soundscapes/id971949061 (Accessed: 01 August 2022).

Audio References	
Spotify	Rain Rain Sleep Sounds. (Version 6.9.3, 2022) *Slow Stream.* [download] Available at: https://apps.apple.com/gb/app/rain-rain-sleep-sounds/id478687481 (Accessed: 23 September 2022). Coast to Coast Recordings (2021) *Mountain Creek.* [download] Available at: https://open.spotify.com/track/5SKs7vPBQ7UOaWsBHu7ljM?si=fe5543bc57d44bb4 (Accessed: 23 September 2022). SleepTherapy (2020) *Soothing Babbling Brook.* [download] Available at: https://open.spotify.com/track/0IyirSFbiXzYXZw1BdgsPI?si=b2f67335724b449c (Accessed: 23 September 2022). Nature Soundscape (2015) *Heavy Flowing Babbling Brook.* [download] Available at: https://open.spotify.com/track/4BZQvFoLYfrBCo9xmn1TiT?si=dafd10063cd84638 (Accessed: 23 September 2022).
YouTube	Nature Soundscapes (17 December 2020) *8HRS Soothing Mountain River Sounds for Sleep and Relaxation - Apshynets River, Carpathian Mountains.* [download] Available at: https://www.youtube.com/watch?v=j6eQUB5LtZA (Accessed: 30 July 2022). BBC Earth Unplugged (18 July 2017) *[Hours Of Relaxing Planet Earth II Mountain Sounds	Earth Unplugged].* [download] Available at: https://www.youtube.com/watch?v=2R2gb0MKJlo10 (Accessed: 30 July 2022). Eric Bartel (11 October 2014) *4 Hours Mountain Stream - Relaxing Nature Sounds.* [download] Available at: https://www.youtube.com/watch?v=Zsqep7_9_mw (Accessed: 25 September 2022).

6 LOCATION SOUNDSCAPE: SEASHORE BY MARGARET MACAFEE

Time to Allow	Topics This Could Be Specifically Useful for
Preparation time: 2 minutes Reflection time: Set a timer	When a client is experiencing turbulent change or overwhelm

I have always found spending time by the sea invigorating. I am drawn to the constancy of the tides while observing the incremental changes wrought to the shoreline with each successive wave. It prompts reflection on time that has passed and all that may await us. The aftermath of a storm at sea reminds us never to underestimate the unpredictability of conditions at sea or the sheer force of its elemental power. Consider also what is revealed when the water retreats at low tide – an inviting sandy beach or potentially treacherous rocky outcrops. This brings future resilience into sharp focus. What uncomfortable truths need our attention? What opportunities are there to strengthen our defences? There is nothing like a contemplation by the sea to restore perspective when a client is experiencing turbulent change or overwhelm. Breathing in synchrony with the ebb and flow of the tide will gradually facilitate a reset.

A pathway for reflection

- Set an intention to reflect upon your clients
- Select a track from the resources provided (or create your own), set a timer (for long tracks) or set the repeat loop (for short tracks) to boundary your reflective space
- Consider the reflective prompts as follows

Reflective prompts

- Focus your attention on the ebb and flow of the waves …
- What are the prominent rhythms or constants in your client's life in this moment? Are they sustainable in the long term?
- How willing is your client to dip a toe in/to get wet feet/ immerse the whole body in new experiences?
- How confident and resilient is your client in the current environment or are they being buffeted by each successive wave?
- When the tide is high on the beach, what vulnerabilities arise?
- When the sea retreats at low tide, what would be exposed?
- If you were to come back in five or even ten years' time, how would the landscape look? What would be familiar and what might simply have been washed away in time?

- What beach defences need to be built to prevent erosion in the long term?
- To close: What is in your awareness now? What feels complete? What needs more attention?

Resources

Create your own seashore Soundscape using myNoise.net.
Available at: http://myNoi.se/IRISHCOAST (Accessed: 22 August 2022).
Available at: http://myNoi.se/TIDAL (Accessed: 22 August 2022).
Available at: http://myNoi.se/PENINSULA (Accessed: 22 August 2022).

Audio References	
iTunes	Félix Blume (2017) '*Waves Crashing on the Beach*', Soundscapes - Listen to Nature. (Version 1.14, 2022). Available at: https://apps.apple.com/app/id1470589737 (Accessed: 30 July 2022).
	Cheryl E. Leonard (No date assigned) '*Pacific Ocean at Tijuana Slough*', Soundscapes - Listen to Nature. (Version 1.14, 2022). Available at: https://apps.apple.com/app/id147058 9737 (Accessed: 30 July 2022).
	Elliot Lang (1994) '*Island Wavescape*', Soundscapes - Listen to Nature. (Version 1.14, 2022). Available at: https://apps. apple.com/app/id1470589737 (Accessed: 30 July 2022).
	Naturespace: Relax Sleep Dream. (Version 5.15, 2020) Infinite Shoreline. [download] Available at: https://apps. apple.com/gb/app/naturespace-relax-sleep-dream/id3126 18509 (Accessed: 1 August 2022).
	Rain Rain Sleep Sounds. (Version 6.9.3, 2022) *Ocean Waves*. [download] Available at: https://apps.apple.com/gb/app/ rain-rain-sleep-sounds/id478687481 Accessed: 23 September 2022).
Spotify	Waveseekers (2021) *Big Pacific Waves*. [download] Available at: https://open.spotify.com/track/5XIpBloItgxw3ARoi AI1eI?si=d247dad436554c9d (Accessed: 23 September 2022).

(*Continued*)

Audio References	
	Coast to Coast Recordings (2021) *Windy Ocean Waves.* [download] Available at: https://open.spotify.com/track/ 6XEEsaEjxwQx4ulaTO1SnT?si=ed1dfd9a6567463a (Accessed: 23 September 2022). KPR Sounds (2021) *Waves Crashing The Beach.* [download] Available at: https://open.spotify.com/track/ 4JPAibfVEbNIDncwz2IEfG?si=60d516d52a954840 (Accessed: 23 September 2022).
YouTube	SleepySounds (8 January 2016) *9 Hours of Waves on a Pebble Beach – Natural White Noise, Sleep Sounds.* [download] Available at: https://www.youtube.com/watch?v=NPSD dUa93kM (Accessed: 30 July 2022). Acerting Art (22 May 2016) *Ocean Sounds (No Music) - Ambient Soundscapes - Sea Waves, Ocean Waves.* [download] Available at: https://www.youtube.com/watch?v= RMNQG8dtWqQ (Accessed: 30 July 2022). LoungeV Films - Relaxing Music and Nature Sounds (24 February 2019) Softest Beach Sounds From the Tropics - Ocean Wave Sounds for Sleeping, Yoga, Meditation, Study. [download] Available at: https://www.youtube.com/ watch?v=B1T06UhcX0Q (Accessed: 31 July 2022).

7 RECORDED MUSIC TO FACILITATE A CHANGE OF RESPONSE BY CLAIRE KITAY

Time to Allow	Additional Resources or Preparation Required	Topics This Could Be Specifically Useful for
Preparation time: 5 minutes Reflection time: 20–30 minutes	Access to Spotify Earphones or headphones Pen/paper for ease and spontaneity of notetaking while listening	When a change of emotional state is needed to bring a new focus or energy to reflection When an ordering or prioritising of different clients is needed, or when a client's needs need grouping and ordering

An awareness of how music can help change my mood has been with me for many years. However, using music more deliberately to aid reflection came when I met Claire Kitay, a music therapist, who supported our Liminal Muse workshops (see pp. x-y). What follows is some guidance from Claire on how you might use music to shift your response to your clients.

Why this approach appealed to me

Listening to music can help to identify and focus on an emotional state. In the context of reflecting on our client work, we may be able to tune in to a mood or emotion projected by a client's issues or to allow our dominant emotion to surface. This exercise might also enable a shift in our emotion or energy such that we feel more focused, prepared or grounded for a subsequent session.

A pathway for reflection

- Set an intention to reflect on your clients. Ideally, something that you feel "biased" about, for example, an assignment you feel particularly proud or disappointed about
- Start track 1, allow yourself to listen and observe the qualities of the music. You might start by noting your response in a non-judgemental manner. Does it make you feel calm? Sad? Heavy? Peaceful? Does it make you tap your foot? Does your breathing change?
- Give yourself five minutes to reflect and finish noting down anything that seems relevant before moving on
- Start track 2, noticing again your physical and emotional responses to the music. Does it enable you to change position, separate from being absorbed into your client's problems and see them from a new perspective? How might this change your thinking and bring new energy to a further session?
- To close: Reflect on this exercise and any notes made, perhaps choose a track you enjoyed as way of creating a boundary to end your reflections

Resources

Please use this QR code to go directly to the playlist.

Kitay, C. M. (2022) *Reflections on Coaching*. Available at: https://open.
spotify.com/playlist/4UEirHoxerAmfc159z1MDH?si=3413ca194
7724c45 (Accessed: 21 July 2022).

List of music as presented in Spotify playlist:

Pro Musica Nipponia (2006) 'Stellar Dream Dances, Op. 98: VII,
Furu-ru', Stellar Dream Dances by Takashi Yoshimatsu. Available
at: https://open.spotify.com/track/3NBmTJcnjPj7BBffRWPefh?
si=7e298721dc184a31 (Accessed: 26 September 2022).

Onix Chamber Orchestra (2017) 'Concerto for 2 Mandolins in
G Major, RV532; III. Allegro', Vivaldi: Mandolin Concertos -
Recorder Concertos. Available at: https://open.spotify.com/track/
42Qj2BT27dHaIpACFitODH?si=67a8dd8465254be6 (Accessed:
26 September 2022).

8 SELF-IMMERSED REFLECTIVE PRACTICE USING SOUNDBATHS BY SUE DAWSON

Time to Allow	Topics This Could Be Specifically Useful for
Preparation time: 5 minutes Reflection time: 30 minutes or more	Where you need permission to pause, be and surrender to what arises To experience how sounds might invite us to become more aware of what occurs emotionally, physically, mentally and spiritually in the moment, or in the quiet after

When we suppress emotions, we stop the natural flow of energy;
sound healing can help by bringing the natural vibration back to

balance. If you think of our energy being like a river running freely, our thought patterns, trauma and suppressed emotions can create a dam in the river. The sound healing gives us the resonance to dismantle the dam giving opportunity for release. Reflection can help us acknowledge what we need to let go to prevent the dam from returning or showing up elsewhere; it is a choice.

Sessions can be crafted using sound psychology to help induce specific brainwave entrainment. For example, dissonant sounds can help to dig in deep and stir up old, rehearsed thoughts or situations giving opportunity for release; harmonising intervals can then help us to let go and surrender and move towards balance. A sacred silence for reflection, "sunyata," is held for several minutes at the end of a soundbath. This is where we meet ourselves without the external sound; it's like we come home to ourselves.

A pathway for reflection

Preparation	• Have your headphones ready with your chosen soundbath selected
	• Lie comfortably to ensure you are warm, perhaps wear an eye mask to shut out other senses. Move your attention to the sounds around you, allowing ALL sounds to be part of the session
Begin (Practice A)	• Engage in some breath work, to help settle and prepare
	• Notice how you are breathing right now …. is it fast, shallow, smooth, slow, faint or loud?
	• Notice how you feel in your mind, settled, distracted, busy or peaceful?
	• Notice how you feel emotionally, label how you feel
	• Notice your body, does it feel soft, fluid, rigid, taught or ache?
	• Come back to your breath, place on your headphones and immerse yourself in the sounds
Sunyata	• At the end, sit in the silence. Observe what shows up?
	• Did you see colours or shapes, gain clarity of thought, gain insights or have dreams and visuals?
	• Did you lose sense of time?

(Continued)

Reflection (Practice B)	• What thoughts do you have about any of that?
	• Consider how you feel **now**:
	    • Physically? Mentally? Emotionally? Spiritually?
	• Take a moment to repeat practice A
	    • What insights did you experience?
	    • Were you able to follow the sounds? Were you distracted or even resisting the sound or practice? What does this tell you?
	    • How did you react to the feelings or thoughts that arose during the session? Did you choose to hang on to them, to judge them or to observe and let go?
	    • How else does that show up in your life?

Close	• What can you do that may help you find more peace and joy in your life? • Come back to your rhythmic breath

Note of Caution: Sound sessions may not be suitable for people with sound epilepsy, severe psychosis and schizophrenia, or for those in the first trimester of pregnancy.

Resources

These are three completely different experiences:

Dawson, S. (2021) '*Gongs and the Well of Dreams*'. Available at: https://insig.ht/F4gc4u5oOsb?utm_source=copy_link&utm_medium=live_stream_share (Accessed: 26 September 2022).

Dawson, S. (2021) '*Reiki and Crystal Bowl Healing Meditation*'. Available at: https://insig.ht/m8TmsL5oOsb?utm_source=copy_link&utm_medium=live_stream_share (Accessed: 26 September 2022).

Dawson, S. (2021) '*Zen Bowl Amidst the Rain*'. Available at: https://insig.ht/spZc8NxqOsb?utm_source=copy_link&utm_medium=live_stream_share (Accessed: 26 September 2022).

A live session of sounds with full percussion into sunyata:

Dawson, S. (2021) '*Retreat Sound Journey – Live*'. Available at: https://insig.ht/44NrRuxqOsb?utm_source=copy_link&utm_medium=live_stream_share (Accessed: 26 September 2022).

Further reading

Goldsby, T. L., Goldsby, M. E., McWalters, M. and Mills, P. J. (2017) 'Effects of Singing Bowl Sound Meditation on Mood, Tension, and Well-Being: An Observational Study'. *Journal of Evidence Based Complementary Alternative Medicine*, 22(3), pp. 401–406.

9 USING MUSIC TO HEIGHTEN AWARENESS AND BRING FOCUS BY CLAIRE KITAY

Time to Allow	Additional Resources or Preparation Required	Topics This Could Be Specifically Useful for
30 minutes	Access to Spotify Earphones or headphones	When either too many or no issues surface as a priority, and a "way in" is sought

When I started the Regular Reflective Practice Space sessions, I used music as a background for other reflective exercises. However, I noticed that sometimes the music prompted more in me than the exercise I had intended to use. In what follows, Claire Kitay, music therapist shares her insight about how to use music as a reflective prompt in its own right.

Why this approach appeals to me

It is almost impossible not to react to music in some way – the use of music in some form to accompany life rituals and social occasions dates back to the earliest human civilisations. Our response to music is located in one of the most primitive areas of the brain. As an example, the unique properties of music can be used to assist in the treatment of many neurological disorders in the formal practice of music therapy. So, using it as a means of bringing the mind to focus or prioritise is a natural and useful step to take.

A pathway for reflection

* Using either one of the sample playlists below or your own, listen to a track

- Notice which thoughts/emotions are coming to the fore most frequently and make a note of this
- Now choose a track which might allow you to reflect on this thought more ...
  - Why is this prominent?
  - Is this the most complex or needy situation in my professional life?
  - Is it in crisis at the moment?
  - Have I pushed this thought down because it seems difficult to address – and the music has brought it to the fore?
  - If you have been feeling "empty," notice what is arising as you listen – is the music helping to awaken a thought or reaction?
  - If nothing arises, what might this suggest to you?
- Allow yourself at least a minute of listening to a track before moving on to a different one. If a quiet/calm track doesn't feel right, try one of the more energising ones and notice your reactions
- Reflect on this exercise and any notes made, perhaps choose a track you enjoyed as way of creating a boundary to end your reflections

Resources

Please use this QR code to go directly to the playlist.

Kitay. C. M. (2022) *Music for Heightened Awareness*. Available at: https://open.spotify.com/playlist/1QTdqec2YuZO7vKo6q9hFz?si=324694ce64bf4be6 (Accessed: 26 September 2022).

List of music as presented in Spotify playlist:

Baroque Chamber Orchestra (1991) 'Canon in D', *Pachelbel's Greatest Hits: Canon in D*. Available at: https://open.spotify.com/track/2tvoY2jAvRY7vaQqhE67Fm?si=3a7d1f908c894f72 (Accessed: 26 September 2022).

Royal Scottish National Orchestra (1999) 'Cantus Arcticus, Op. 61, Concerto for Birds and Orchestra: II Melankolia', *Cantus Arcticus/Piano Concerto No.1/Symphony No.3 by Rautavaara*. Available at: https://open.spotify.com/track/0hlm68qctRvvh2d493B3R3?si=649e0cb3bb784ae7 (Accessed: 26 September 2022).

National Symphony Orchestra (2020) 'Tempest (the Music of Chaos)', *The Mythos Suite by Debbie Wiseman*. Available at: https://open.spotify.com/track/5lQtaE9ma2wcL5sAbyoNye?si=cb7e1b5baa1a43be (Accessed: 26 September 2022).

Pink Floyd (2014) 'Side 2, Pt. 3: Unsung', *The Endless River*. Available at: https://open.spotify.com/track/6St7hjIG2njuG5Zck8vK4Q?si=fcb11a695ce54e59 (Accessed: 26 September 2022).

National Symphony Orchestra (2020) 'Voyage of Scyrus (the Music of Sysiphus)', *The Mythos Suite by Debbie Wiseman*. Available at: https://open.spotify.com/track/2oGfb2awMfYsj3rwqZcZOH?si=b37ebf8440874487 (Accessed: 26 September 2022).

Emerson String Quartet (1991) 'String Quartet No.17 in B-Flat Major K.458 "The Hunt":III. Adagio', *Mozart: The "Haydn" Quartets*. Available at: https://open.spotify.com/track/1HMUX9dDGW0HiByM4ePupZ?si=6f52aae7349b4345 (Accessed: 26 September 2022).

10 WEATHER SOUNDSCAPE: THUNDER BY MARGARET MACAFEE

Time to Allow	Topics This Could Be Specifically Useful for
Preparation time: 2 minutes Reflection time: Set a timer	When a client is navigating difficult emotions or conflict with others around consequential issues

Like many people, I am somewhat fearful when I witness the flash of lightning that heralds an impending thunderstorm. The instinct is to dash to a place of safety and shelter while the rumbles of thunder echo, ominously, in the distance. Sitting with our discomfort, we can appreciate the dramatic release of energy that cools a febrile atmosphere. It mirrors the energetic forces that collide in a conflict after a period of simmering dissent. Expressing such difficult emotions will ground us, much like earthing of the current generated when lightning strikes the soil. In a split second, lightning also illuminates the night sky, offering us the prospect of fresh insight or a creative spark. When we next venture out after a storm, we can immediately feel the refreshing breeze and a dip in temperature. It may cause us to reflect on the root cause of the tensions and feel emboldened to address them sooner.

A pathway for reflection

- Set an intention to reflect upon your clients
- Select a track from the resources provided (or create your own), set a timer (for long tracks) or set the repeat loop (for short tracks) to boundary your reflective space
- Consider the reflective prompts as follows

Reflective prompts

- Imagine you are sitting with your client on a wooden veranda, sheltered from the incoming storm
- Begin by noticing the lightning as bolts dart towards the ground ...
- In that moment, what might be illuminated for your client?
- What tensions or emotions have been building up, ready to be sparked?
- Draw your attention now to the rumbles of thunder as they travel across the sky ...
- How might the thunder mirror the pressures exerted on your client? What might be bubbling just below the surface, requiring the perfect set of conditions to precipitate a storm?
- How prepared are they to face a storm? Will they be energised by the drama or fearful of the consequences?

- What shelter can they find to ride it out? Who or what might provide haven and for how long?
- Consider the increasing intensity of the rain and how that affects their immediate landscape …
- What are they learning as they endure the extremes of this weather event? How are they changing?
- Have they experienced the cleansing after-effect of the storm – the fresher air, the reduction in heat and humidity? What is the potential for re-emergence?
- To close: What is in your awareness now? What feels complete? What needs more attention?

Resources

Create your own Thunder Soundscape using myNoise.net.
Available at: http://myNoi.se/THUNDER (Accessed: 22 August 2022).
Available at: http://myNoi.se/THUNDER2 (Accessed: 22 August 2022).
Available at: http://myNoi.se/STORM (Accessed: 22 August 2022).

Alternatively, access one or more of these suggested tracks:

Audio References	
iTunes	Félix Blume (2018) *'Storm at Night'*, Soundscapes - Listen to Nature. (Version 1.14, 2022). Available at: https://apps.apple.com/app/id1470589737 (Accessed: 15 June 2022).
	Elliot Lang (2016) *'Erie Thunderstorm'*, Soundscapes - Listen to Nature. (Version 1.14, 2022). Available at: https://apps.apple.com/app/id1470589737 (Accessed: 30 July 2022).
	Rain Rain Sleep Sounds. (Version 6.9.3, 2022) *Thunder Cracks*. [download] Available at: https://apps.apple.com/gb/app/rain-rain-sleep-sounds/id478687481 (Accessed: 21 September 2022).
	Rain Rain Sleep Sounds. (Version 6.9.3, 2022) *Crashing Thunder*. [download] Available at: https://apps.apple.com/gb/app/rain-rain-sleep-sounds/id478687481 (Accessed: 21 September 2022).

(Continued)

Audio References	
Spotify	Thunderstorms (2022) *Thundering Storm*. [download] Available at: https://open.spotify.com/track/4FCYUt UTeB6CgsdJMnQIL4?si=76620a89d1b44b9b (Accessed: 20 September 2022).
	Loud Thunder Sounds | Sounds of Thunder and Rain (2020) *Deep Thunderstorm - Loopable*. [download] Available at: https://open.spotify.com/track/2iMC95aR0IDIVSWmUjsFpf?si=b8ad38fb0a604c42 (Accessed: 20 September 2022).
	Nature Sounds (2012) *Healthful Rolling Thunder With Distant Rumble*. [download] Available at: https://open.spotify.com/track/34n0Ecmkfdxlejb6R3VzLL?si=a0b02ac4d28f4537 (Accessed: 20 September 2022).
YouTube	Relaxing Guru (5 May 2021) Violent Thunderstorm Over a Tent in Africa | Rain, Thunder & Lightning Sounds for Sleeping, Relaxing. [download] Available at: https://www.youtube.com/watch?v=QQv2nmj82lw (Accessed: 31 July 2022).
	Stardust Vibes – Relaxing Sounds (12 April 2017) Heavy Thunderstorm Sounds | Relaxing Rain, Thunder & Lightning Ambience for Sleep | HD Nature Video. [download] Available at: https://www.youtube.com/watch?v=gVKEM4K8J8A (Accessed: 31 July 2022).
	Danny Louis (4 October 2021) Goodbye Insomnia With Heavy Rain & Thunder Growls on a Stale Tin Roof in Foggy Murky Forest at Night. [download] Available at: https://www.youtube.com/watch?v=sfn3lnBolFo (Accessed: 31 July 2022).

11 WEATHER SOUNDSCAPE: RAIN BY MARGARET MACAFEE

Time to Allow	Topics This Could Be Specifically Useful for
Preparation time: 2 minutes Reflection time: Set a timer	When a client is experiencing a prolonged period of difficulties and needs support to shift their perspective and alleviate self-criticism or self-doubt

I find a gentle and consistent rain soundscape to have a calming, often meditative quality. I can almost sense the rain on my skin and at my feet. Rain has long been associated with cleansing and renewal. A burst of rain can clear away pollution and dust, while delivering vital rejuvenating water to all forms of life. It also serves to disrupt our normal routines – requiring extra clothing, perhaps a different mode of transport and certain a degree of resilience, if one is getting thoroughly soaked. There will be times when we positively embrace the disruption and others when it serves to reinforce a more downbeat assessment of life. We might berate ourselves for being insufficiently prepared but, in doing so, become over-burdened with metaphorical waterproofing and back-up plans. Sometimes, we realise that getting wet serves a purpose and, eventually, the clouds part and the sun will shine once again.

A pathway for reflection

- Set an intention to reflect upon your clients
- Select a track from the resources provided (or create your own), set a timer (for long tracks) or set the repeat loop (for short tracks) to boundary your reflective space
- Consider the reflective prompts as follows

Reflective prompts

- Imagine that you and your client are caught together in this rain …
- How would they be reacting to the simple fact of getting wet? What would they be noticing? Would they be embracing the sensation of rain on their face, head and clothing?
- Would they have come prepared for rain? Or would they immediately want or need to run for shelter?
- Under what circumstances could they be persuaded to just enjoy getting drenched? What could they discover from this form of letting go?
- What role might a periodic downpour have on their practice? Could it offer life-giving moisture to enrich their ecosystem?
- When is there too much rain? What steps could they take to capture or extract what they need (like a water butt) while

preventing unwanted damage due to flooding? Do they perform regular checks on their infrastructure to ensure preparedness?

- How will they feel when the rain stops? What will they look forward to when the clouds part and the sun begins to shine again?
- To close: What is in your awareness now? What feels complete? What needs more attention?

Resources

Create your own rain Soundscape using myNoise.net.
Available at: http://myNoi.se/RAIN (Accessed: 22 August 2022).
Available at: http://myNoi.se/RAIN2 (Accessed: 22 August 2022).
Available at: http://myNoi.se/RAIN3 (Accessed: 22 August 2022).

Alternatively, access one or more of these suggested tracks:

Audio References	
iTunes	George Vlad (2019) '*Calm Rain in the Borneo Rainforest*', Soundscapes - Listen to Nature. (Version 1.14, 2022). Available at: https://apps.apple.com/app/id1470589737 (Accessed: 25 September 2022).
	Elliot Lang (2016) '*Gentle Rain and Bird Songs*', Soundscapes - Listen to Nature. (Version 1.14, 2022). Available at: https://apps.apple.com/app/id1470589737 (Accessed: 30 July 2022).
	Naturespace: Relax Sleep Dream. (Version 5.15, 2020) *The Indigo Raindrop*. [download] Available at: https://apps.apple.com/gb/app/naturespace-relax-sleep-dream/id312618509 (Accessed: 1 August 2022).
	Rain Rain Sleep Sounds. (Version 6.9.3, 2022) *Rain Downpour*. [download] Available at: https://apps.apple.com/gb/app/rain-rain-sleep-sounds/id478687481 (Accessed: 21 September 2022).
Spotify	In Natura (2021) *By the Trees at the Boathouse*. [download] Available at: https://open.spotify.com/track/34Z5XQxU2hqGuN6BWU0gB4?si=a2cc1c465e7f4615 (Accessed: 20 September 2022).

Audio References	
	Epic Soundscapes (2020) *Heavy Rain*. [download] Available at: https://open.spotify.com/track/7rQ1E6bl6UMhrRhf 8quVIR?si=b22ff83448f64eeb (Accessed: 20 September 2022).
	Rainfall (2022) *Crisp Clear Rain*. [download] Available at: https://open.spotify.com/track/2DNqc7Q27oZYHTX 3OL04Lj?si=81e4fd045391434e (Accessed: 25 September 2022).
YouTube	Relaxing White Noise (15 October 2020) *Here Comes the Rain (Sounds) Again. Rainstorm White Noise for Sleeping or Focus*. [download] Available at: https://www.youtube. com/watch?v=Xoc8I5m_eao (Accessed: 15 June 2022).
	Rain and Chill (25 August 2019) *Gentle Rain Falling on Leaves in the Rainforest	Nature Relaxing Sounds for Sleep, Insomnia, Stress*. [download] Available at: https://www.youtube. com/watch?v=Qj0Mbs9hwsk (Accessed: 1 August 2022).
	MeditationRelaxClub – Sleep Music & Mindfulness (13 October 2012) *Rain Sounds 10 Hours: The Sound of Rain Meditation, Autogenic Training, Deep Sleep, Relaxing Sounds*. [download] Available at: https://www.youtube. com/watch?v=jX6kn9_U8qk (Accessed: 3 August 2022).

12 WEATHER SOUNDSCAPE: WIND BY MARGARET MACAFEE

Time to Allow	Topics This Could Be Specifically Useful for
Preparation time: 2 minutes Reflection time: Set a timer	When a client is directing or impacted by systemic change

I am drawn to wind soundscapes when curious about the flow of energy within a system, the strength of that flow and the direction of travel. If we are in alignment with a system, we might think of having "the wind at our back," conferring a supportive nudge in our desired direction. Conversely, working against the system means we represent an obstacle and will be buffeted until we submit, move aside or manage to influence the direction of travel. The impact of wind can range from the refreshingly benign (a caressing breeze) to the highly destructive (a tornado or hurricane). Our ability to reduce the negative consequences of those more extreme weather events depends on the meteorological intelligence we can access, alongside the long-term planning decisions for our critical infrastructure. To prevail in the storms that life presents, we can keep an eye on the horizon, chart critical data points and plan strategically to shore up our defences.

A pathway for reflection

- Set an intention to reflect upon your clients
- Select a track from the resources provided (or create your own), set a timer (for long tracks) or set the repeat loop (for short tracks) to boundary your reflective space
- Consider the reflective prompts as follows

Reflective prompts

- Imagine your client being buffeted by powerful gusts of wind …
- Did the wind arrive unexpectedly? Is it stronger than forecasted? Does your client need to "batten down the hatches" for a while?
- What forces are at play? What is at risk should this state continue?
- What fears might such turmoil generate? Are there opportunities to seize amidst the turbulence? Is this disruption to their flow beneficial in the long term?
- What will enable them to withstand a seemingly relentless wind? What serves to strengthen them and where might they be exposed or vulnerable?
- How likely are they to soar with the extra energy in the air and the wind at their back? How would it feel for them to be fully untethered and simply embrace the thermals?
- What assumptions have been uprooted by the storm, like an ancient tree or young sapling?

- To close: What is in your awareness now? What feels complete? What needs more attention?

Resources

Create your own Wind Soundscape using myNoise.net.
Available at: http://myNoi.se/WIND (Accessed: 22 August 2022).
Available at: http://myNoi.se/DESERTWIND (Accessed: 22 August 2022).
Available at: http://myNoi.se/DESERTSTORM (Accessed: 22 August 2022).

Alternatively, access one or more of these suggested tracks:

Audio References	
iTunes	Franscisco López (2000–2003) '*Wind (Patagonia)*', Soundscapes - Listen to Nature. (Version 1.14, 2022). Available at: https://apps.apple.com/app/id1470589737 (Accessed: 15 June 2022).
	Claude Schryer (2018) '*Leaves Tickle*', Soundscapes - Listen to Nature. (Version 1.14, 2022). Available at: https://apps.apple.com/app/id1470589737 (Accessed: 15 June 2022).
	Rain Rain Sleep Sounds (Version 6.9.3, 2022) *Desert Wind*. [download] Available at: https://apps.apple.com/gb/app/rain-rain-sleep-sounds/id478687481 (Accessed: 21 September 2022).
	Rain Rain Sleep Sounds (Version 6.9.3, 2022) *Blizzard Wind*. [download] Available at: https://apps.apple.com/gb/app/rain-rain-sleep-sounds/id478687481 (Accessed: 21 September 2022).
Spotify	Calmsound (2016) *Wind Sounds: Strong Wind Through Orchard Trees*. [download] Available at: https://open.spotify.com/track/0m08WL2WTUoWa5zdd14qSE?si=c205ba06024b441a (Accessed: 20 September 2022).
	Nature Sounds (2016) *Deep, Arctic Wind Sounds*. [download] Available at: https://open.spotify.com/track/5F2hfrn2OZf1emasBiKnL0?si=911587b3a3444f71 (Accessed: 21 September 2022).

(*Continued*)

Audio References	
YouTube	Nature Sounds (2012) *Peaceful Sustained Shimmering Wind.* [download] Available at: https://open.spotify.com/track/5TDQ7rG2hz3TqYvCVfAysB?si=651464c4fe894fdd (Accessed: 21 September 2022). Relaxing Sounds of Nature (30 March 2018) *Strong Howling Wind Sound 2 Hours/Swaying Spruce Trees in The Wind.* [download] Available at: https://www.youtube.com/watch?v=sT5f1jBJHng (Accessed: 31 July 2022). Relaxing Soundzzz (12 February 2018) *Winter Storm Ambience With Icy Howling Wind Sounds for Sleeping, Relaxing and Studying Background.* [download] Available at: https://www.youtube.com/watch?v=sGkh1W5cbH4 (Accessed: 15 June 2022). Relaxing Sounds of Nature (26 March 2018) *Relaxing Sound of Howling Wind Blowing Sand/Relax, Sleep, Stress Relief, ….* [download] Available at: https://www.youtube.com/watch?v=V8sjMUBz_M0 (Accessed: 01 August 2022).

Anecdotes from practitioners using auditory prompts

Ocean Sounds – (No Music) – Ambient Soundscapes – Sea Waves, Ocean Waves

What shifted as a result of the exercise?

Generally, I do not enjoy the writing of notes following a coaching call and I found that in approaching reflection through auditory exploration, my notes were succinct and more focussed.

How did you feel about the reflective experience?

I find being near, and hearing the sea, soothing and it transforms me to an open/creative state so the Seascapes were my "go to." I love the sounds of nature so any of the others could easily have been chosen.

As I opened it in YouTube, I was initially watching the waves then closed my eyes. This shifted my awareness, allowing my mind to roam and then focus. I found myself able to experience, and process, from multiple perspectives.

Karen Charles, Senior Support Advisor, NABS: Reflective Practice Participant, August 2022.

Binaural beats

What shifted as a result of the exercise?

It's immersive. The outside world was shut out for ten minutes and my often hectic mind was channelled in one direction, rather than many. This in turn left more space to apply meaning in this reflective space.

How did you feel about the reflective experience?

There was a bit of a learning curve with binaural beats, but once past that stage of figuring out what it's about and experimenting I found a tonal beat that provided an environment of focus. It blocked out the outside world and the reflections began. I used good quality over-ear headphones, and whilst this level of kit isn't available to everyone, I would encourage people engaging with this activity to get their hands on the best pair of headphones they have to enhance the experience.

SB, EMCC Accredited Coach at Senior Practitioner Level; Director at Jemco Consultancy Ltd.

6

KINAESTHETIC PROMPTS TO AID REFLECTION

AN INTRODUCTION TO REFLECTING WITH KINAESTHETIC PROMPTS

In the prompts that follow I have emphasised approaches that are more somatic i.e. things that engage the body more than the mind. Some of the exercises involve leaving your workspace and using the outdoors. If you choose one of these experiments, please take appropriate measures so that you are both comfortable and safe.

Some of the exercises are playful and childlike. This is intentional as I believe play is a helpful route to explore more of who and how we are. In this quote from Winnicott (2005, pp. 72–73), he suggests:

"It is in playing and only in playing that the individual child or adult is able to be creative and to use the whole personality, and it is only in being creative that the individual discovers the self."

On occasion, the reflective prompt invites you to use materials that you might feel are incongruent with your professional identity. We encourage you to notice these responses as they could offer rich territory for exploration. The renowned phrase of Thomas à Kempis, published in Latin in the 1400s and translated into English by Reverend W. H. Hutchings in 1881, was made in the context of human suffering "You cannot escape it, run where you will; for wherever you go, you take yourself with you, and you will always find yourself." I offer it here, because should you feel uncomfortable with some of the suggested prompts, it might be useful to explore what it is that creates this discomfort. Generally, the prompts are intended for

DOI: 10.4324/9781003311188-7

reflection on your client work and your relationship to it. However, when you notice a strong reaction to them, this can be an invitation to explore your preferences, bias and assumption. Ultimately this could have pertinence for your whole life, not just your clients.

Within the kinaesthetic prompts, there are often cognitive components. Many of us default easily to "thinking things through" and where that brings insight, you may feel that this is sufficient. However, the prompts in this section are intended to stimulate more than your thinking ability, encouraging you to engage with your fullest way of being in the world. Perhaps paradoxically you cannot "will yourself" into being more holistic – rather it requires a gentle compassion to notice your default, to hold it lightly such that more will reveal itself.

A mindfulness exercise to help you prepare for reflecting with kinaesthetic prompts

- You may find it helpful to stand for this exercise, or if you prefer to be seated, then ensure your feet can connect with the floor
- Bring your attention to your breath
- Notice how the air enters your body and how it leaves again
- Place your attention on your feet – consider how they connect with the surface beneath you. Perhaps rock your feet, one at a time, slowly forward and then back, notice you're your muscles and tendons move, notice the temperature of the floor ... experience your sensations fully
- Continue to breathe slowly and purposefully such that you feel stable and solid in your connection with the ground
- Taking the time that you need, move your attention slowly upwards through your body, heightening your awareness of what sensations are asking to be noticed
- For each sensation, welcome it on an in-breath, then on an out-breath acknowledge it and move on
- If you have a tendency to rush, joints offer obvious places for a pause. Rest and take a couple of breaths when you get to your ankles, knees, hips, wrists, shoulders and neck
- When you reach your neck and head, see how far upwards you can experience sensations – can you feel your scalp, your hair?
- Reverse the body scan moving from your head back down to your feet, do so more swiftly while keeping a gentle appreciation of what is asking to be noticed

- Perhaps something needs an energetic release, perhaps something needs additional savouring? Give your body the attention it is asking for
- Gently repeat the body scan upwards and downwards a few times more, such that you feel in tune with your whole self
- Finally, take a couple of deeper resourcing breaths before continuing with the reflective prompts

References

Hutchings, W. H. (1934) *Of the Imitation of Christ in Four Books.* London: Longmans, Green and Co.

Winnicott, D. W. (2005) *Playing and Reality.* Abingdon: Routledge.

1 CONNECTING WITH NATURE BY LOUISE SCHUBERT

Acknowledgements: Abigail Heathcote and Pauline Greystone

Time to Allow	Topics This Could Be Specifically Useful For
Preparation time: 5 minutes	When you have a particular question to explore
Reflection time: 15 minutes or more	When you want to bring a freshness to your habitual way of thinking or working

Louise shared with me a sparkling moment having facilitated this exercise. I loved the idea of taking inspiration from our natural surroundings. Additionally, if we are looking to widen our perspective, then being open minded about what alternative prompts may offer, feels like a congruent approach. What follows is based on Louise and her colleagues experience with groups, adapted for independent reflection.

Why this approach appealed to me

I developed this as a supervision exercise for two teams of social workers. The very demanding work carried out by these professionals, supporting youth with special needs, at the edge of society; meant that self-care was a recurring theme during our sessions.

After five virtual sessions, permission was given to meet in person. The meetings occurred as we emerged from the restrictions of the COVID-19 lockdown. I wanted to find a powerful exercise to celebrate the opportunity that we had to come together in nature, to provide space for individual reflection and to share our insights as a group. The exercise served its purpose, magic occurred, tears of emotions were shared as answers were found in the beautiful space. I often now send this to clients for private reflection.

A pathway for reflection

- Choose a place for this experience that you sense might hold a positive energy for you – somewhere in the open air, perhaps a park, a beach, or a woodland ...
- Bring a question to which you seek an answer, trust whatever question comes to you spontaneously
- Perhaps carry a small notebook to capture anything which seems important, alternatively trust that whatever is important will stay with you
- Place your attention on your breath ... take three or five deep breaths
- Notice your feet connecting with the earth ...
- Moving slowly, rotate 360° to absorb the nature around you
- Take time to enter the reflection, feel it with all your bodily senses, your soul and your heart
- Start walking; look for a place that invites you along the way, where some answers may appear. Consider ... What does this space know about my question/topic? Look at your surroundings as if it were for the first time, view things with a beginner's mind
- Stay a while ... take a 360° view, consider "What else does this space know about my question/topic?"
- If you choose to, take photos or draw in the notebook. Pick up something you find, a stone, a leaf, a twig that inspires you, and that will remind you of this moment. If no damage is done to nature, take the object with you. Alternatively, take note of what you leave behind as you move to another place. Before leaving, consider ... "What will be the name that I give to this space?"

- Continue with the path and find another place to repeat the whole process
- When you are ready to close the exercise, return to your starting point, consider … What do you know now?

Further reading

James L. and Way, M. (2017) *Insights in Space*. Great Britain: Clean Publishing.

Patterson, E. (2019) *Reflect to Create!* Milton Keynes, UK: Lightening Source UK Ltd.

Prentice, K. (2019) *Nature's Way*. Milton Keynes, UK: Lightening Source UK Ltd.

2 DARING TO BE BY CLAIRE DAVEY

Time to Allow	Topics This Could Be Specifically Useful For
Preparation time: 5 minutes Reflection time: 30 minutes or more	Useful to explore self as instrument, to consider who and how we are as we work Useful when you are stuck and want to gain a different perspective and tap into an innate wisdom of what lies beneath

Why this approach appealed to me

I've always found it a challenge to conform to traditional forms of reflection, and over the years I have discovered creative alternatives to great effect. Being schooled in many types of yoga, it's the restorative and yoga nidra elements of practice that I've found offer a deep reflective and nourishing space. This state of being has been full of surprises and you get to lie down to experience it!

I'm reminded of the Taoist Proverb "We cannot see our reflection in running water. It is only in still water that we can see." So, this meditative self-enquiry, is an invitation to pause, be still and just be.

A pathway for reflection

- **Settling in** – get comfortable laying down or sitting if preferred. Ensure you are warm enough as your body temperature is likely to drop. Maybe have something supporting your head and under your knees if lying down. Have a notebook to hand
- **Setting an intention** – create this in sentence form e.g. "I welcome and am enquiring into … my core emotions/assumptions/judgements in relationship with … ." Repeat it three times.
- **Journey of attention** – move your attention around your body starting with the right-hand thumb and each finger, left hand, then toes on right and left, finishing with the chin, lips, tip of tongue, nostrils, eyes, forehead, whole of head, whole of body
- Bring awareness to the breath and **breathe** rhythmically and smoothly, counting down slowly from 11
- **Exploring polarities:**

  - Notice any emotions that arise. What's dominant? Where does this emotion reside? Really sense into it, always welcome what emerges
  - What's the opposite of this emotion? Where does it reside?
  - How might you sense and switch between these polar emotions?
  - How might you sense into them simultaneously?
  - Repeat the process for any emerging assumptions or judgements that might be calling your attention, always welcoming in what emerges

- Return attention to the breath. On the inhalation, breath in compassion and on the exhalation, breathe out and release the body into the moment
- Feel back into the body by bringing gentle movement to your fingers and toes
- When you are ready, capture what emerged along with your conclusions and actions as a result

Resources

Dare to be (2022) Available at: www.DaretoBe.Global.

Yoga Nidra Network (2022) *Yoga Nidra Library*. Available at: https://www.yoganidranetwork.org/nidras/. (Accessed: 23 September 2022).

Further reading

Dinsmore-Tuli, U. and Tuli, N. (2022) *Yoga Nidra Made Easy: Deep Relaxation Practices to Improve Sleep, Relieve Stress and Boost Energy and Creativity*. UK: Hay House.

3 EMOTIONS BODY MAPS

Time to Allow	Topics This Could Be Specifically Useful For
Preparation time: 5 minutes Reflection time: 15 minutes or more	When trying to articulate or clarify an emotion that you witness in yourself or your client When wanting to acknowledge an emotional experience before releasing it

Why this approach appealed to me

I discovered this research when supervising a team of phone support workers who were noticing an increased emotional intensity in their caller's situations. As an empathic group of people, the team were struggling to hold an impartial frame and so asked to bring this to supervision.

The researchers, Nummenmaaa et al. (2014) proposed that emotions are represented in the somatosensory system (i.e. our bodies). Over 700 participants across the globe engaged in a range of self-report experiments. The outcome was this universal series of emotional heat maps in Figure 6.1.

Given emotions are a subjective experience, these maps offer a way of sharing our emotions with others. The more activated an area of the body, the more red and yellow the area on the body map. The more de-activated an area the more black and blue the corresponding area on the body map. So, rather than labelling the

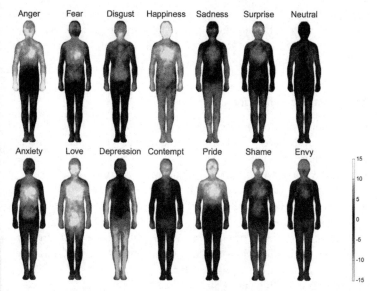

Figure 6.1 Body maps showing regions whose activation increased (warm
colours) or decreased (cool colours) when feeling each emotion

Note: A full-colour version of this figure, as well as animated body maps of emotions, are
available at the website of the Human Emotion Systems laboratory, University of Turku:
https://emotion.utu.fi/media/.

emotion we have experienced (which others may interpret differently), we can share how we experience the emotion in our bodies
(which the research suggests is a more universal understanding).

Models of embodied emotion suggest that we understand
someone else's emotions by simulating them in our own bodies
(Keysers et al., 2010; Niedenthal, 2007). In professional supervision,
the concept of the parallel process recognises this and we then explore how a complementary energy might be played forward when
next with our client.

With this team, I invited them to connect with some of the
emotions in Figure 6.1. Then we considered what body maps they
experienced when talking to their callers – sharing what was similar
and different amongst the team. My intention was to help them
accept their emotional responses rather than control them. To move
us to close, it felt important to locate a resourceful state. Given their

desire to remain impartial with callers, I asked them to draw this as a body map. The idea being that they might more easily access this bodily state when they became drawn into the emotional components of their caller's narrative.

A pathway to reflection

- Recall a client situation which you would like to understand more fully. Do so in as much detail as you can, as though bringing the client into your space
- Shift your attention to your bodily sensations, which parts of you feels more activated, which parts feel deactivated?
- Cast your eyes across the bodily emotion maps as a reference if that seems helpful
- What's your sense of where those emotions have come from … from your client? From you? From the "us" that has been created in relation to each other?
- Where does this take you?
- In the context of your client, what needs to happen next?
- To move to close: pick a body map (or create your own) of an emotion that you would like to experience now. Re-enliven a moment which helps you embed those sensations

Resource

Nummenmaa Lab: Human emotions systems laboratory (no date). Media. Available at: https://emotion.utu.fi/media/. (Accessed: 19 September 2022).

References

Keysers, C., Kaas J. H., and Gazzola, V. (2010) 'Somatosensation in social perception', *Nature Reviews Neuroscience,* 11(6), pp. 417–428.

Niedenthal, P. M. (2007) 'Embodying emotion', *Science,* 316(5827), pp. 1002–1005.

Nummenmaaa, L., Glereana, E., Harib, R., and Hietanend, J. K. (2014) 'Bodily maps of emotions', *The Proceedings of the National Academy of Sciences,* 111(2), pp. 646–651.

4 FOREST BATHING BY JO BOND

Time to Allow	Topics This Could Be Specifically Useful For
Preparation time: 5 minutes Reflection time: 15 minutes or more	When you need to re-centre yourself prior to doing more reflective practice When the context in which you are operating marginalises self-care and you want to resource yourself such that you bring generative energy into a depleted system

Jo is a frequent attendee on our Reflective Practice Space sessions. Once she shared that she'd had a morning Forest Bathing. There was a freshness and vibrancy to her energy, I was intrigued! As this is Jo's discovery, I have invited her to share her experiences and to explain how it can be used, with or without a forest.

Why this approach appealed to me

Forest bathing was on my radar given my biology degree and fascination with the natural world. I was intrigued whether this activity could enhance my restorative practice to ensure that I am in the best mental, physical and emotional place for my coachees. The Forest Bathing Institute was offering an introductory workshop at Kew Gardens, near my home. It was a transformational experience that engaged all of my senses and rebalanced and re-energised me that day. I found it a powerful, holistic, and somatic approach to achieving deep, creative reflection and I now use it regularly, especially if I have experienced challenging emotions in my clients.

A pathway for reflection

- Where possible, take your senses outside to a green place – you do not need to be in a forest, you can use a garden, park or anywhere where there are trees. You can also gain benefits from plants on a balcony or house plants
- Schedule this practice when you can be uninterrupted. Even 15 minutes can provide benefits

- Stay open without prejudging expectations
- Start to walk slowly and mindfully without any pre-planned route
- Breathe deeply through your nose, making your outbreaths longer
- Look at the scenery, regarding trees at different distances and from various angles to exercise your eyes and enhance observation. What colours do you see?
- Listen to the natural sounds around you e.g. wind, rain, water. Are there any sounds from the surface you are walking on?
- Sit or lean against a tree and connect to the textures and shapes
- What are the scents and smells around you?
- Are you aware of any taste sensations?
- Focus on your mind – what thoughts, themes and ideas arise for you?
- Focus on your body – how does it feel? What is happening to your pulse rate?
- Focus on your emotions – how's your mood?
- Now move your attention to your clients and note what arises

Resource

The Forest Bathing Institute (2022) *What we do*. Available at: https://tfb.institute/. (Accessed: 19 September 2022).

Further reading

Li, Q. (2019) *Into the Forest: How Trees Can Help You Find Health and Happiness*. UK: Penguin Life.

Miyazaki, Y. (2018) *Shinrin-yoku: The Japanese Art Forest-Bathing*. Oregon: Timber Press.

Natural England (2021) *Official Statistics: The People and Nature Survey for England (April–June 2020)*. Available at: https://www.gov.uk/government/statistics/the-people-and-nature-survey-for-england-adult-data-y1q1-april-june-2020-experimental-statistics. (Accessed: 19 September 2022).

5 HELICOPTERS AND CHAIRS

Time to Allow	Topics This Could Be Specifically Useful For
Preparation time: Find some plasticine or similar Reflection time: 15 minutes or more	Generating distance and alternative perspectives to review your work Using your physical stance to enrich reflection

Why this approach appealed to me

This approach blends two of my favourite approaches; the seven-eyed model (Hawkins and Smith, 2006) and mapping the system (Urschel, 2020). The seven-eyed model reminds me that when engaging with a client there are at least seven perspectives from which to make sense of things. So, in choosing one (probably my favourite), I inevitably miss six others.

In reflection I sometimes map my notes on a schematic of the seven-eyed model which helps me notice what I might have missed. This feels sedentary and is typically done in the same chair from which I did the work. By combining the model with systemic mapping whilst integrating movement, it liberates energy as well as greater ease in taking alternative perspectives.

The schematic in the Figure 6.2 contains 11 elements. Depending on the issue, I might not include every element. Some are naturally oriented inwards and others outwards to the wider world.

A pathway for reflection

- Take 11 sheets of A4 paper, label them with the elements in Figure 6.2. Change the terminology to suit your context – so, client might be coachee or patient or team member
- Consider which of the elements you would like to explore; start with 3 or 4
- Place the paper around the room. What makes sense to you? This may or may not be similar to the layout of Figure 6.2

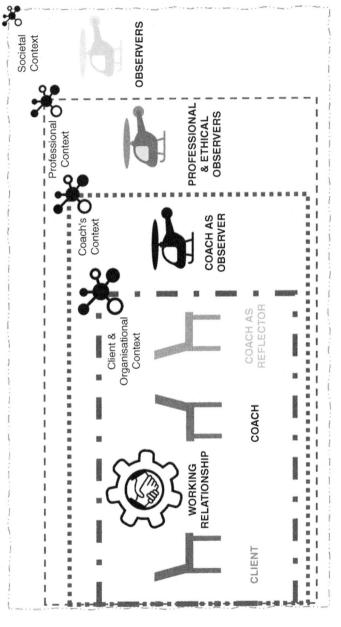

Figure 6.2 Helicopters and chairs

- Stand in a neutral place i.e. not on a piece of paper. Take a mindful moment, to feel grounded
- Move slowly to one piece of paper. If it is a chair, then "step on" and stay for a while. If it is a helicopter, then "hold on" to it and move slowly with it
- Enliven your understanding of how things feel here and now. How balanced do you feel? Which parts of you feel hot, warm, cool? Where is your knowing in this moment – intellectual, emotional, spiritual? Stay (or move slowly) a while longer and see what else might be asking for attention. What do you not yet know …?
- When you feel ready, "step off" the paper or "let go of" it and return it to its original position. Now shake off the energy (just like a dog shakes the rain off its fur …)
- See which element calls you next. Perhaps you want to move the papers? Perhaps you want to exchange some? Do what you feel is needed. Repeat the on and off process again
- Repeat this as often as feels helpful. Return to a neutral space and consider:

  - What's with me now?
  - What's with others now?
  - What's gone now?
  - What am I grateful for now?

- To close: gather up, file or dispose of the papers in a way that feels respectful

References

Hawkins, P. and Smith, N. (2006) *Coaching, Mentoring and Organisational Consultancy: Supervision and Development.* Maidenhead, UK: Open University.

Urschel, M. D. (2020) 'Mapping what is', in Lucas. M. (ed.) *101 Coaching Supervision Techniques, Approaches, Enquiries and Experiments.* Abingdon: Routledge, pp. 279–281.

6 LEVERAGING MOTION

Time to Allow	Topics This Could Be Specifically Useful For
Preparation time: 5 minutes Reflection time: 15 minutes or more	Useful when you recognise there is a need for preparing for or processing after a session Helpful to deliberately review your whole portfolio

Why this approach appealed to me

The roots of this approach emerged through happenstance. For example, when employed, I used the commute to prepare for the day ahead, and to review what happened. When building my coaching practice this habit accompanied me as I drove to and from a client. Similarly, on long car journeys, I'd review my business development pipeline. While my intention was commercial, often the memory of a particular client would spark something. I'd forget about the pipeline and get curious about my client's progress.

My coach training coincided with me working in central London, and so I used the commute to fulfil the requirement to journal my practice clients. When my writing stalled, I'd look out the train window, somehow that prompted more.

My twice daily dog walk mirrors the daily commute – I can prepare and distil as I move. I find this useful for planning; where I have an idea for a service or product, the forward motion seems to offer encouragement. I notice a difference when there is no rush, a slower pace brings a meditative quality, allowing me to be with myself.

I suspect many of us will ruminate on these occasions; however, here I deliberately use motion for reflection. The pathway below brings intention and purpose to these opportunities such that you leverage motion which is part of your life, in service of your clients.

A pathway for reflection

- Consider where motion is a natural part of your routine e.g. a commute, a journey or exercise

- What do you naturally do when you are in motion, and what would happen if you left space for something else to occur?
- Set an intention to reflect on your clients. For example:

  - Set a positive frame and actively think about things that have gone well
  - Pose a more curious frame and re-visit any niggles that you noticed
  - Take a methodical approach, review your client list one by one and consider how you are with them
  - Be prepared to free-wheel – simply notice what comes up
  - Consider your next supervision session, how might you use it

- Capture your reflections safely, perhaps a voice recording on your mobile device
- Schedule a review to see which kind of motion enhances your reflections
- Design some more focused experiments and then hone this over time

7 OUR HUMANITY@WORK: THE 7CS LENS FOR INSIGHT, LEARNING AND CHANGE

Acknowledgment: Elaine Patterson

Time to Allow	Topics This Could Be Specifically Useful For

Preparation time:
  5 minutes
Reflection time:
  15 minutes or more
	Client situations which trigger effortful interventions on your part
	Or when you might have lost your open warm-hearted connection with yourself or your client, when you might be feeling stuck or judgemental, when you need to reconnect with your humanity, or when something human, humane, new or different beyond technical models is needed

Elaine and I have never worked together and yet through an awareness of her approaches, I feel I almost know her. I was drawn to her model about

Figure 6.3 The 7Cs self-assessment map

the 7 C's (See Figure 6.3) *as it encourages us to reflect soulfully yet in an evaluative way. Here Elaine shares a little of her intention for this concept.*

Why this approach appealed to me

I wanted to move beyond technical and cognitive approaches to design a reflective lens that would help us embrace our shared human condition and our shared humanity soulfully and whole-heartedly when we work.

The beauty of the 7Cs is that I have seen them as innate heart-based qualities which are therefore available to us at any time – if we choose – to invite them when we work. The lens bypasses our head brain to helps us to explore the depths of who we are, who we are becoming and how this shows up with others. The lens is very flexible and can be used in any context from the personal to the systemic on any question.

When I use the lens, I work holistically with all of the 7Cs to discover what is working, what is missing and what is needed. I am always surprised by what is revealed and what wants to emerge!

A pathway to reflection ...

- Consider the definitions of the Seven Capacities provided (Patterson, 2020, p. 9)
- Linger on each capacity in turn, taking time to understand not just what this means to you at a cognitive level, rather where you experience that capacity in your body
- Some of the capacities may be experienced more keenly than others – make a note using the numbers within the diagram to capture your base line ratings
- Bring a client scenario to mind ...
- Re-visit the Seven Capacities diagram, tuning into your somatic self. Without over-thinking, notice:

  - What capacities are you drawn to?
  - Which capacities feel neutral or absent?
  - How might you rate each one when you are with this particular client?

- What has emerged? What information has arisen that might be useful for your client practice?
- Revisit the Seven Capacities diagram one final time. For you to return to your baseline, what might you need to let go of, accept, or welcome?

Reference

Patterson, E. (2020) *"Our Humanity@Work" Working with the 7Cs – the 7 Human Capacities – for Insight, Learning and Change: A New Lens for Coaching, Coaching Supervision and Executive Reflection.* London: The Centre for Reflection and Creativity Limited.

Further reading

Patterson, E. (2015) 'What Are Leaders' Experiences of Reflection? What Leaders and Leadership Developers Need to Know From the Findings of an Exploratory Research Study', *Reflective Practice*, 16(5), pp. 636–651.

Srivastava, P. S. (2016) 'Spiritual Intelligence: An Overview', *International Journal of Multidisciplinary Research and Development*, 3(3), pp. 224–227.

8 REFLECT TO CREATE! BY ELAINE PATTERSON

Time to Allow	Topics This Could Be Specifically Useful For
Preparation time: 5 minutes Reflection time: Anything from 15 minutes to an hour or more	Situations where we need to find the courage to be with ambiguity and our not knowing, bringing a soulful compassion to ourselves and others to creatively embrace what wants to emerge, igniting our imaginations, firing our agency and giving us hope

Why this approach appealed to me

Grounded in research, "Reflect to create!" is a holistic labyrinthine philosophy and choreography which invites us to find (or reclaim) our own humanity and our own freedom for inspired living and great work, so that we may resource others to do the same. Questions are explored through the metaphor of the dance, identifying four moves, namely the Prelude, The Opening, The Flow and The Denouement (with its 9 supporting dance moves and 199 different creative practices). See Figure 6.4.

"Reflect to create!" draws from fields of adult learning, mindfulness, relational dynamics, psychology, systems perspectives, creativity, the Arts and from Nature. It is an invitation to explore what makes us clumsily, delightfully and elegantly human in our quests. It is the bedrock of my own life and work, I hope you enjoy working with its myriad of invitations too!

Figure 6.4 Reflect to create: The dance of reflection

A pathway to reflection

[N.B.: This is an abridged version, see Further Resources for more information.]

Linger on each as you need taking time to feel into each of the questions with our heart, body and soul. Circle back as often as you need.

- Start with "The Prelude" – the work before the work. Taking your journal, scrapbook or sketchbook ask:

  - What is your question? Do you have an image or a picture that represents this for you?
  - What makes you vulnerable with your question? Where does this vulnerability show up in your body?
  - What permissions or generous acts of self-compassion can you offer yourself as you explore your question?

- Now move into "The Opening"

    - Suspending: "What might you need to let go of now?"
    - Seeing anew: "Where is your curiosity and wonder taking you now?" and "What are you sensing?"
    - Relating to the whole: "What new connections or relationships are you sensing?', "What is the bigger context here?"

- Now move into "The Flow"

    - Initiating the invitation: "What new invitations are here now?"
    - Art of listening: "What are you listening for?" and "What is now emerging from the dark?"
    - Finding freedom: "What does your soul want you to know right now?" and "What does space and freedom look and feel like right now?"

- And finally, now move into "The Denouement"

    - Crafting focus: "What needs to be crafted?" and "What needs to be tested?"
    - Working wisely: "What discernment is needed?" and "As you move forward how can you attend to the wellbeing of the whole?"
    - Feeding forward: "How will you know you in harmony with life?"

Resources

Patterson, E. (2019) 'Reflect to Create!' The Dance of Reflection for Creative Leadership, Supervision and Reflective Practice. London: The Centre of Reflection and Creativity Ltd.

Patterson, E. (2019) 'Reflect to Create!' The Dance of Reflection for Creative Leadership, Supervision and Reflective Practice – Reflective Journal and Workbook. London: The Centre of Reflection and Creativity Ltd.

Patterson, E. (2022) Reflect, Create, Inspire. www.elainepatterson executivecoaching.com/retreats. (Accessed: 19 September 2022).

Reference

Patterson, E. (2015) 'What Are Leaders' Experiences of Reflection? What Leaders and Leadership Developers Need to Know from the Findings of an Exploratory Research Study', *Reflective Practice*, 16(5), pp. 636–651.

Further reading

Prelude to the dance by Oriah Mountain Dreamer (2018) Available at: http://www.personalpassages.com/wisdom/poems/prelude-to-the-dance/. (Accessed: 27 September 2022).

9 REFLECTIVE MOVEMENT BY SUE DAWSON

Time to Allow	Topics This Could Be Specifically Useful For
Preparation time: 5 minutes Reflection time: 30 minutes or more	Improving your somatic awareness and using reflective practice to ease the body and mind In the moment practices

Why this appealed to me

Have you ever paused to think that your body may reflect what you think on a subconscious level? In my work, my intention is to help people be aware of the possible links between how the body feels and what information any discomfort holds. Through giving attention to simple movements and noticing how our bodies respond, we have an opportunity to connect body and mind to bring awareness of further emotional work that needs to be done. Perhaps by being more connected with our bodies we release stuck energy and find new ways of being with our emotions.

You may have noticed how your body responds when you have had a stressful day. If you are feeling tired, withdrawn, or exhausted your body may fall forward, the heart feels heavy and the chest falls inward. Shoulders may hike and move towards the ears, like you are shutting out the world, the noise. Conversely, when you have had good news or feel amazing, you may have noticed, quite literally, a spring in your step, your heart feels light and your arms and legs swing more freely.

While ageing may bring its share of aches and pains it can be interesting to consider what psychosomatic information our body holds. In my experience emotional injuries can create negative energy which gets stuck in the body and can change the way we think, behave and move. For example, clients experiencing pain in the shoulders, are often taking on the responsibilities of others as if they were their own. Stiffness in the hips can relate to not feeling free to move forward, perhaps holding back from life to avoid pain. Those experiencing constant coughing or sore throats, tight jaw, grinding teeth may also be struggling to hear or speak their own truth.

The practice which follows invites you to listen more deeply to your body and consider what meaning you make of its messages.

A pathway for reflection

- Stand up, and just allow your body to wiggle and jiggle freely, then explore just moving around
- How does that feel … silly … uncomfortable … fluid … expressive?
- See if you can totally let go and let the body flow …
- What do you notice … perhaps some parts of you move freely and some don't?
- What connections might you make between how you are feeling in this very moment and what has been going on around you recently, or maybe something from way back …?

Further reading

Dawson, S. (2022) *Reflective Practice: Your Body Is a Reflection of Your Thoughts and Emotions*. Available at: http://www.sensegreaterpeace. co.uk/blog/reflective-practiceyour-body-is-a-reflection-of-your-thoughts-and-emotions. (Accessed: 26 September 2022).

Doidge, N. (2016) *The Brain's Way of Healing: Stories of Remarkable Recoveries and Discoveries*. London: Penguin.

Van der Kolk, B. (2015). *The Body Keeps the Score: Mind, Brain and Body in the Transformation of Trauma*. London: Penguin.

10 SHAPING MODELLING CLAY

Time to Allow	Topics This Could Be Specifically Useful For
Preparation time: find some plasticine or similar Reflection time: 15 minutes or more	Useful when something you feel a need to use your physical self to work something out

Why this approach appealed to me

In reading Jo Birch's 2022 book I was inspired by her creativity. I decided to experiment too, asking a group to bring Play-Doh, or plasticine to the next session. My local retailer had neither, so I purchased a slab of modelling clay. I invited the presenting supervisee to fiddle with their plasticine as they shared their client situation, the rest of the group did similarly as we listened. We then revealed our creations. Interestingly, some of the group created recognisable forms and objects, some created abstract forms. Without really thinking about it, the supervisee had formed a ring with five spikes on it, one was larger than the rest ... interestingly there were five people in her client situation. See Figure 6.5.

Opinion was divided about how we might integrate this into our own practice – perhaps some clients might see these materials as too child-like. I also realised why plasticine was recommended, modelling clay creates a powdery mess! The supervisee had used Blu-Tac; this felt like a professional alternative. Subsequently I purchased some pink-tac, to signpost it is not for sticking up flip charts. When I am at my desk, and I notice a client or colleague conversation is occupying me, I'll pick up the pink-tac, letting my thoughts emerge. Somehow it creates a greater sense of deliberation and purpose for meanderings that might otherwise diffuse.

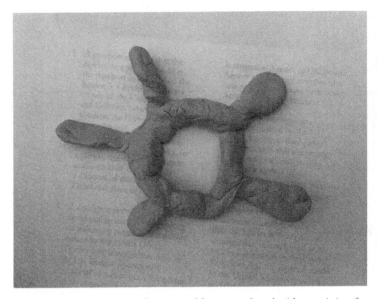

Figure 6.5 Representation of a group of five, reproduced with permission from Anita Hayne, Coach and Coach Supervisor

A pathway for reflection

- Take the modelling material in your hands and manipulate it so that you can feel its texture and its plasticity
- Bring to mind a moment to reflect upon
- Perhaps model the material to create individual forms for each element in the situation, or perhaps mould it randomly as you continue to reflect
- Pause – observe what you have created through this process, what might this illuminate? Would it be helpful to arrange the pieces a particular way?
- Pause again – how do you feel about the situation, are you still holding your responses in your body or are they now located in the clay?

Reference

Birch, J. (2021) *Coaching Supervision Groups: Resourcing Practitioners.* Abingdon: Routledge.

11 USING TEXTURES TO EXPLORE BY LIZ FORD

Time to Allow	Resources Needed	Topics This Could Be Specifically Useful For
5–10 minutes (to gather a variety of textures)	A variety of things you can hold and touch. These might be cool, warm, smooth rough, bumpy, prickly, rubbery, silky …	Bringing a different perspective to a situation you don't quite understand
15 minutes or more for reflection	Pen and paper to capture thoughts	Accessing a desired state

Why this activity appealed to me

In my own reflections, I have noticed how using more unusual, less well used techniques have brought new insight to my work. This technique was developed in response to clients who mentioned a particular interest in textures and were keen to explore what hidden knowledge might be uncovered through tactile responses.

Over time I have realised that certain textures reliably generate resourcing energy for me. For example, holding a cold, smooth, heavy, glass paperweight can help me feel more centred and less likely to be drawn into any drama. Therefore, a variation of the approach below is to simply sit with your chosen texture, connecting in it in such a way as to access a desired state.

Some of the questions offered below are drawn from Clean Language which I find useful for exploring without assumption.

A pathway for reflection

- Decide what you'd like to reflect on
- Look at the textures you assembled
- As you think of the issue, what textures seem to fit the situation? Gather those together
- Now take time to sit with each of the chosen textures, perhaps close your eyes to heighten your sense of touch

  - Holding it lightly

- Passing it from hand to hand
- Turning it over or stroking it as you ponder
- Noticing how it feels
- Not thinking too hard, just letting thoughts emerge

- What is it about this texture that fits?
- What does each texture tell you about the situation?
- Now consider which textures do **not** fit the situation. Gather those together

  - Take time to feel each texture and consider why it **doesn't** fit the situation you are exploring
  - What is it about these textures that do not fit?
  - What does each texture tell you about the situation?

- Now consider what solutions/resolutions are emerging

  - Which textures fit best with these?
  - What is it about these textures that help?
  - What do they know about the solution to your issue?
  - And what do you know now?
  - And what actions do you want to take a result of that knowing?

Further reading

Karpman, S. (1968) 'Fairy Tales and Script Drama Analysis'. *Transactional Analysis Bulletin*, 7(26), pp. 39–43.

Sullivan, W. and Rees, J. (2008) *Clean Language: Revealing Metaphors and Opening Minds*. Carmarthen: Crown House Publishing Limited.

12 WALKING REFLECTIONS BY LIZ FORD

Time to Allow	Resources Needed	Topics This Could Be Specifically Useful For
30 minutes plus	Appropriate clothing and footwear for the weather and terrain chosen Pen and paper/phone to capture thoughts and evocative scenery	Feeling stuck Sensing a need for movement Needing a break and a fresh perspective

Why this activity appealed to me

I try to walk every day and notice it clears my mind. Over the years I've found my clients like being outdoors too, so I often take them walking. It's good to get away from computers and offices and into somewhere more resourcing. This technique draws on the environment to inspire new thinking, stimulate awareness and make connections. It can be used in countryside, parkland and city streets.

A pathway for reflection

- Decide what you want to reflect upon and pose it as a question to yourself
- Choose where to walk
- Begin by tuning into your whole body as you walk

    - Notice the feel of the ground beneath your feet
    - Acknowledge any tension anywhere in your body and ease it out as you walk
    - Consciously pay attention to each of your senses in turn. What are you seeing, hearing, smelling and feeling?
    - All this should help you move into a greater sense of somatic awareness

- Now think of your reflection question and hold it lightly in your mind as you walk
- After about 5 minutes, bring your awareness to the pace you have slipped into and consider how this links with your reflection question. How congruent does it feel?
- Now try walking at a faster pace for about 5 minutes and see how that feels. How does the faster pace connect or jar with your reflection question?
- Now slow things right down to a very leisurely, relaxed pace for a few minutes. How does this slower pace impact your reflections?
- Finally, take time to stop and notice in more detail what is happening around you, remember to look up as well as around
- What new feelings/thinking does this stopping and this noticing bring?

- As new thoughts arise you might like to jot them down or take a picture of the thing/place that inspired them
- When you get back to your starting point, take time to notice what's shifted, identify insights and learning and capture any resulting actions

Further reading

Oppezzo, M. and Schwartz, D. L. (2014) 'Give Your Ideas Some Legs: The Positive Effect of Walking on Creative Thinking', *Journal of Experimental Psychology: Learning, Memory and Cognition*, 40(4), pp. 1142–1152.

National Trust (no date) *A beginner's guide to forest bathing.* Available at: www.nationaltrust.org.uk/lists/a-beginners-guide-to-forest-bathing. (Accessed: 19 September 2022).

Street Wisdom (2022) *Inspiration on the go.* Available at: www.streetwisdom.org. (Accessed: 19 September 2022).

Anecdotes from practitioners

Working with the 7C's

What shifted as a result of the exercise?

Everything was mid-range between 4 and 7! I was especially uncomfortable with Courage due to a project and me not giving my experience a voice. Since then, I have provided feedback and agreed a transition period to end my role. The start of my journey emerged here! Contemplation was also uncomfortable, and I realised that this was a frequency, rather than a competency, issue; when I did it, I did it well, I didn't do it often enough. Since the session, I make weekly opportunities to contemplate, especially in nature and whether walking or sitting, and always on my own.

How did you feel about the reflective experience?

This activity sat well with me. I liked the colourful layout of the 7Cs – human capacities or qualities – and could easily annotate my reflections. I have progressed and now am work free on Mondays and Fridays as first surfaced here.

RPS Participant October 2021

Shaping modelling clay

What shifted as a result of the exercise?

I was reflecting upon an exchange where I felt I may have caused the other person to feel "less than" and was wondering how I might repair any damage. Observing myself working with the play-doh I was reminded of my own patterns, my preference for thinking and logic. I wondered what patterns had been in force with this person – and quickly spotted my tendency to become more directive when I feel under time pressure. I thought about whether I would do the same again next time – in truth, probably yes. That felt unpalatable, and yet it really did feel like I had no other choices. Something clicked, it did *feel like* there were no other choices, but of course that wasn't actually true. In that moment something shifted. I felt lighter, I knew I wanted a conversation with her, I needed to do some reparation, and while I still had no clue about what else I might have done, I became curious to discover what choices she saw, that I had missed.

How did you feel about the reflective experience?

I felt strangely child-like as I chose this prompt to work with, to begin with I just liked the way the play-doh felt in my hands, I noticed it's smell which evoked childhood memories. I had to remind myself that this was about my practice. As I thought about the situation, I noticed how I was very much in my head and was "logic-ing" what I "should" create. I looked out of my window, replaying the situation, and continued to fiddle with the play-doh. I created three separate pieces. Reaching the end of my reflections I wondered what meaning they held. For two of them, nothing really resonated, the third piece, looked a little like a bird in flight. Perhaps a reminder not to hold onto things too tightly and to know when to let them go.

RPS Participant, September 2022

7

POETRY TO AID REFLECTION

AN INTRODUCTION TO REFLECTING WITH POETRY

As you engage with this section, we invite you to put to one side your current relationship with poetry. Perhaps like me, you remember being schooled to remember an impenetrable poem simply to prove that you could. Alternatively, you may continue to enjoy stimulation from the words of your favoured poet. Here we invite you to begin again, to bring a fresh curiosity to how poetry might inform your reflective practice.

There are many poetic forms, rhythm and rhyme, ballads, blank verse and even limericks. Indeed, Flanagan (2019) observed that "perhaps the characteristic most central to the definition of poetry is its unwillingness to be defined, labeled or nailed down." He continues … "Poetry is the chiseled marble of language. It is a paint-spattered canvas, but the poet uses words instead of paint, *and the canvas is you.*" Indeed, it is the potential of poetry to trigger a subjective response which feels useful when we are seeking out reflective prompts.

We invite you to look beyond the literal and to notice what is evoked in you. As Keats is believed to have said "A poem needs understanding through the senses. The point of diving in a lake is not immediately to swim to the shore; it's to be in the lake, to luxuriate in the sensation of water. You do not work the lake out. It is an experience beyond thought. Poetry soothes and emboldens the soul to accept mystery" (cited in Brehm, 2017, p. 188).

The kind of poetry which appeals to each of us is highly personal and situational. What appeals to one person, irritates another.

DOI: 10.4324/9781003311188-8

Further, our reaction to a poem on one day may be quite different to our response to the same poem on another day. So, when reading each poem do so lightly – you may feel open or resistant. Trust your response; it holds information. Should you choose to, you could challenge yourself to stay with the poem even when you are inclined to turn away. The experience of doing so will also reveal information.

What follows are 12 poems that I have deliberately chosen, some of which have prompted deep reflection in me. However, all of them have been offered to participants in my Regular Reflective Practice Space (RPS) sessions and have had a profound impact on at least a handful of people. So, my hope is that across the chapter you will connect with poems that offer useful reflective prompts for you. When the poem offered has had a strong impact on me, I will include the questions or thoughts it prompted to illustrate how it might impact you. By way of example, below you will also find some anecdotes from RPS participants sharing how a poem impacted on their reflective practice.

Our selection for this book cannot possibly reflect the rich range of poetic material available. Perhaps you already have some favourite poems, in which case you may find it useful to develop your own library specifically for reflection. Additionally, we offer a number of poems in this section which are hereto unpublished and have been written by practitioners in the field. We hope this inspires you to consider creating poetry for yourself.

For those who are not used to using poetry as a prompt for reflection, there is a suggested pathway for reflection. This is not the only way, part of the experimentation is to discover how to use poetry in a way that is useful for you.

A pathway for reflection

- Set an intention to read the poem in service of your clients
- Read the poem for the first time, perhaps read it aloud, so that you absorb what it holds
- Pause: Notice the impact of the poem for you – remember there are no should's here, only how it is
- Without rushing, read the poem again and notice which passages you are drawn to …

- If you feel inclined, stay with those passages a while – settle into the words …
- Consider what questions or thoughts arise in you, prompted by the poem and which may be of relevance to your client work …
- Capture what you need to sustain your ongoing reflections

References

Brehm, J. (2017) *The Poetry and Impermanence, Mindfulness, and Joy.* US: Wisdom Publications.

Flanagan, M. (2019) *What Is Poetry, and How Is It Different?* Available at: https://www.thoughtco.com/what-is-poetry-852737 (Accessed: 11 August 2022).

1 A DEEPER MEETING BY HENRY CAMPION

Time to Allow	Topics This Could Be Specifically Useful for
Reading time: 2 minutes	Meditation prior to a session
Reflection time: 15 minutes or more	Reflecting on our presence during or after a session

The poem: "A deeper meeting"

I awaken to this space
the sights, the sounds
the gift of now

this flow of breath
this beating heart
this skin that tingles

I scan for tensions
release each one
slip back into the flow

I open my heart
to a wider world
where all are one

Sitting before you
the space between us
resonates with being

Touched by humility
I let go of agendas
accept not-knowing

I see you, listen deeply
as you speak your truth:
memories shift

old certainties fray
time-served narratives
lose their grip

At last you're free
to re-shape your story
find new ways to be

A pathway for reflection

See pages 161–162.

Why this poem appealed to me

Henry narrated a version of this poem at a colleague's book launch – I was hooked. He read it slowly, which allowed us to bathe in it. I asked him to share it with me. The version here is one that he uses as a meditation, before meetings. The words were inspired by Gregory Kramer, the Buddhist monk and originator of "Insight Dialogue," a form of interpersonal mindfulness practice, and the work of Daniel Siegel, psychiatrist and neuroscientist.

So, this poem (or meditation) has practical value for me in helping me become more present in the moment. In addition, conceptually it helps me to look beyond my skills and competencies and to immerse myself in whatever is happening and emerging through the client and myself in our being together.

The passage that speaks most to me is

Sitting before you
the space between us
resonates with being

It brings a sense of fullness and richness to that which exists imperceptibly between two people who have come together to reflect and enquire. When I get caught up in performance anxiety, when my imposter comes out to take a few swipes at me – it is this notion of a space "resonating with being" that settles me. I become curious about "us" and about the "other" and about who I am when I am part of "us" – I am able to wonder … What will we discover together?

References

Campion, H. (2020) 'A Deeper Meeting', *Coaching Perspectives*, 26, p. 14.

Kramer, G. (2007) *Insight Dialogue: The Interpersonal Path to Freedom.* US: Shambhala Publications Inc.

Siegel, D. (2012) *Pocket Guide to Interpersonal Neurobiology: An Integrative Handbook of the Mind (Pocket Guides)*. New York: W. W. Norton & Co.

2 CONNECTED BY MARIE QUIGLEY

Time to Allow	Topics This Could Be Specifically Useful for
Reading time: 2 minutes Reflection time: 15 minutes or more	Capturing the essence of all or part of a session

The poem: "Connected"

Purposeful like a Panther
Courage in the ring
To Call Forth in a loving, open hearted practice
Inviting us all to sing

Vulnerability in motion
That 'niggle' asking for more
The posing of a question
Allowing our creativity to soar

The learning and the growing
As the music plays
The depth of reflection powers
Our choice to stay.

A pathway for reflection

See pages 161–162.

Why this appealed to me

This was written by Marie Quigley, at the close of a supervision group, in response to my invitation to capture learning. Remarkably she wrote this in three and a half minutes while listening to a piece of music! As she shared her creation with the group, I was moved by its messages and completely flummoxed as to how she wrote something so beautiful so swiftly. Marie is not a practiced poet – however, I know her as someone who speaks easily from her heart.

I include this poem to encourage you, the reader, to find the poet in you. I asked Marie to share how she brought these words into being, which I hope will ignite a poetic spark. Here are her thoughts …

> *On the invitation to reflect, I took some deep breaths and as I listened to the music, I closed my eyes and brought all members of the group along with the cases and topics we discussed into my awareness. As I re-lived the experience, I was able to observe the whole session in my mind's eye. The flow of the music enhanced my senses. Clear images and metaphors emerged as I watched the session unfold and this followed on with the formation of words. The words felt like they came from my heart. I felt playful, joyful and deeply connected to the group and to my inner self. I wrote the words as they appeared in front of me. I didn't question if anything made sense and wrote freely. The title came after I read the whole piece to myself.*

3 *EACH OF US IS LIKE ONE DROP OF RAIN* BY NICHOLAS GORDON

Time to Allow	Topics This Could Be Specifically Useful for
Reading time: 2 minutes Reflection time: 15 minutes or more	Responding to feelings of isolation or insignificance Considering how serendipity has affected where we are today

The poem: "Each one of us is like a drop of rain"

Each of us is like one drop of rain,
A single splatter on the thirsty sand.
Remember, though, that drops fall not alone,
The products and producers of a grand
Harmony that waters well the plain.

Do not think, then, that you're on your own,
A tiny drop upon a dying land.
You are a storm, whose green fields will remain.

A pathway for reflection

See pages 161–162.

Why this appealed to me

I discovered this poem while researching this book and found Nicholas Gordon prolific in his generation of poems and generous in openly sharing them through his website. He intends them for personal use, so we were sure to get his specific permission for this one.

It was difficult to choose, so I enlisted the support of some colleagues. I chose a handful of poems that I had "noticed" as I perused his site. However, everyone had different preferences. To resolve the indecision, I rolled a die – a four – this poem was fourth in the list.

Now that it is "here" I'm able to give it some proper attention. I remember why I noticed it in the first place. The experience of living through a pandemic has meant that many of us feel alone; indeed, many of us were quite literally alone, and yet we were not alone in this experience. I made the connection between this and his metaphor of a drop of rain, which is in fact a part of a storm.

I'm also struck by the serendipity of the poem finding its way through to this book. Writing this at a time when there is unrest amongst our European neighbours makes me grateful for the happy accident of being born in the UK.

The poem's first letter of each line spells "Earth Day" and the poem's theme is about the environment. The final three lines remind me that each of us makes a contribution, however small, which collectively can make a significant impact.

Reference

Gordon, N. (2009) *Each One of Us Is a Drop of Rain*. Available at: http://www.poemsforfree.com/eacho3.html (Accessed: 17 May 2022).

4 EARTH, FIRE AND WATER BY WILLIAM YEATS

Acknowledgement: Linda Aspey

Time to Allow	Topics This Could Be Specifically Useful for
Reading time: 5 minutes Reflection time: 15 minutes or more	Exploring the continuum of directive and non-directive practice Reviewing assignments with clients who struggle with self-acceptance

The excerpt from: "Earth, Fire and Water"

We can make our minds
So like still water
That beings gather around us
That they may see, it may be
Their own images,
And so live for a moment
With a clearer, perhaps even with a fiercer life
Because of our quiet

A pathway for reflection

See pages 161–162.

Why this appealed to me

I first met this poem when training in the Time to Think philosophy with Linda Aspey. It was part of the training manual and supported the notion that one of the most important things we can do as a practitioner is to give our fullest Attention (one of Nancy Kline's ten components of a thinking environment) to our client.

In researching this book, I discovered it is not a standalone poem, but an excerpt from a story (which I find a little baffling!). However, for me, Yeats words are a reminder that our own thoughts and processes can cloud our ability to offer a true mirror for others. When we ground ourselves and leave space for the other, it liberates them to fully explore their own truth.

I continue to find these words inspiring and when I find myself being more "noisy" than I intended, the metaphor of the "still water" helps me relocate my quieter self. I also find it a great reminder that when with clients who lack confidence, it is most helpful if we park our desire to rescue and find a way of letting them see their personal power independently.

References

Kline, N. (2002) *Time to Think: Listening to Ignite the Human Mind.* Cassell: London.

Yeats, W. B. (1893) 'Earth, Fire and Water'. Reproduced in *The Celtic Twilight: Faerie and Folklore (2017),* Independently Published, p. 39.

5 FIRE BY JUDY BROWN

Time to Allow	Topics This Could Be Specifically Useful for
Reading time: 3 minutes Reflection time: 15 minutes or more	Work–life balance Wellbeing Loosening our need for control

The poem: "Fire"

What makes a fire burn
is space between the logs,
a breathing space.
Too much of a good thing,
too many logs
packed in too tight
can douse the flames
almost as surely
as a pail of water would.
So building fires
requires attention
to the spaces in between,
as much as to the wood.

When we are able to build
open spaces
in the same way
we have learned
to pile on the logs,
then we can come to see how
it is fuel, and absence of the fuel
together, that make fire possible.

We only need to lay a log
lightly from time to time.
A fire
grows
simply because the space is there,
with openings
in which the flame
that knows just how it wants to burn
can find its way.

A pathway for reflection

See pages 161–162.

Why this appealed to me

My previous supervisor offered this as a resource to our group. Although it was triggered by a broader discussion, its messages stayed with me. I love watching a real open fire and so this also gave me a sense of warmth and connection. Then at a time when I had too much to do and too little time to do it in, I remembered the poem and read it more purposefully.

We were in lockdown, everything was packed into the same physical space and I was fatigued. These words resonated

> *"When we are able to build open spaces in the same way we have learned to pile on the logs, then we can come to see how it is fuel, and absence of the fuel together, that make fire possible."*

They impacted upon me at two levels. Firstly, a reminder to build space for myself and not just provide space for my client. Plus, it was at the start of the Regular Reflective Practice Space programme, so it felt congruent with my belief that we all need to remember to build open spaces in which things can emerge.

Reference

Brown, J. (2016) *The Sea Accepts All Rivers and Other Poems*. USA: Trafford. pp. 34–35.

6 LIMINAL PLACES BY CHARLOTTE HOUSDEN

Time to Allow	Topics This Could Be Specifically Useful for
Reading time: 5 minutes Reflection time: 15 minutes or more	Exploring transition Engaging with uncertainty and ambivalence

The poem: "Liminal Places"

Liminal – a space
In between.
The transition from
One stage to the next.

Leaving past lives
Behind, but
Not arriving
somewhere else yet.

From light into darkness,
Then back into light.
Verge of mind, heart and body.
The noise becomes quiet.

Places uncertain, flimsy,
Unsettling or exciting.
Landing born of the
Mindset we're holding.

Liminal – a hallway,
An existence on edge.
We're not what we were,
Not yet what we'll be.

It might be a gap
Into which we can step.
A place where we could
Truly be free.

A pathway for reflection

See pages 161–162.

Why this appealed to me

Charlotte and I collaborated to develop her images (known as Liminal Muse) as catalysts for deeper coaching conversations. We facilitated workshops that helped people explore their responses to transitions they were facing. In advertising the workshops, Charlotte crafted a paragraph that was already quite poetic. I asked her to "convert" this into a poem for this book – and I absolutely love the outcome. For me, the following phrase honours my aspirations to progress my practice which at the same time will require me to re-define my professional identity.

We're not what we were,
Not yet what we'll be.

In the workshops, Charlotte explained liminality as the place "in-between" – for example, when a trapeze artist has let go of one swing and has not yet grasped the next. It has the potential for provoking anxiety – yet simultaneously, this is our opportunity to fly. Exactly how I feel about my current learning edge.

7 METAMORPHOSIS (IN THE FLOW) BY DAVID CROWE

Time to Allow	Topics This Could Be Specifically Useful for
Reading time: 5 minutes Reflection time: 15 minutes or more	Exploring how we are responding to our current life chapter Re-evaluating what priorities we hold

The poem: "Metamorphosis *(in the flow)*"

Growing more comfortable day by day in my lined, bearded 50+ skin
I'm doing more of the things I like doing, seeing more of the people I like seeing
Writing, poetry, music, meditation have ceased to be strangers and becoming companions
Happy with a diet of enough work that is meaningful, clear weekends, dinner with a friend
Joy of the universe through the lens of close up, the small canvas of
A sunny day, a wry observation, stroking the cat, a family that intuits love, support and fun.

Saying goodbye to big socials, dinner parties, and the false bonhomie of drink
Nights out with habitual friends who feign interest but really want the entire spotlight
The few close that mutually bind is enough
Rolling through the bad times not so deep and not so long
With a deep conviction that that sun will shine again.

My Dad gone, my Mum lost in illness, the wider family dispersing, it is
time to grow up
To further build the internal reservoir of peace, to look after the
ageing body
Have some adventures and travel, to carry on learning
Maybe make some surprise friendships and connections along the way
Listen to my heart more than my head
And trust that I love myself and those around me, hold the right
things dear.

A pathway for reflection

See pages 161–162.

Why this appealed to me

That I am writing this book is a reflection of my current life
chapter – one which puts more emphasis on play and less on
work. It is a transition that is proving harder than I imagined.
Having invested so many decades in building a career and then
an independent practice, I had little knowledge of what spare
time was or how I should use it. It is a familiar challenge for
those who don't want to "retire," rather to continue to their
professional practice while using their time in a more blended
way.

I am fortunate to be part of a small group of colleagues all
transitioning towards a fulsome life in our advancing years. This
poem was written by one of the group about his own transition.
I was drawn to his growing acceptance of the ageing process and
his sense of re-calibration of what we choose to hold as important
in our lives. Both of which are very much a "work-in-progress"
for me.

Further reading

Colston, T. (2018) *Retireista*. UK: Retireista.

8 NINE TYPES OF SILENCE BY PAUL GOODMAN

Time to Allow	Topics This Could Be Specifically Useful for
Reading time: 5 minutes Reflection time: 15 minutes or more	Exploring silence within a session Exploring your own relationship with silence

The piece

> *"Not speaking and speaking are both human ways of being in the world, and there are kinds and grades of each. There is the dumb silence of slumber or apathy; the sober silence that goes with a solemn animal face; the fertile silence of awareness, pasturing the soul, whence emerge new thoughts; the alive silence of alert perception, ready to say, 'This ... this ...'; the musical silence that accompanies absorbed activity; the silence of listening to another speak, catching the drift and helping him be clear; the noisy silence of resentment and self-recrimination, loud and subvocal speech but sullen to say it; baffled silence; the silence of peaceful accord with other persons or communion with the cosmos."*

A pathway for reflection

See pages 161–162.

Why this appealed to me

I came across this quote when I was reflecting on a group session that had ended with silence. The core of the supervision dialogue had finished and we had ten minutes until the official end. I remember feeling uncertain – had I missed something? Should I fill the space? Should I wait for someone else to fill the space? Is it OK to sit with the silence? I deferred to the group – some people chose to leave and some stayed. That felt OK.

I often offer a resource by way of follow up and this quote resonated with my experience. It seems to me that a single word cannot express the multiple nuances that are experienced when we are not speaking. I notice that Goodman's (1973) articulation truly honours those differences.

Now, when I am with a client and silence is with us, I remember these words. I become more curious about which of the nine silences it might be, and in doing so, my attention is drawn more deeply towards my client. I worry less that I may have done something "wrong," my tendency for impatience subsides, my compassion for both myself and the client rises. I find myself willing to wait, gently, for whatever comes next.

Reference

Goodman, P. (1973) *Speaking and Language: The Defence of Poetry*. London: Wildwood House Ltd.

9 START CLOSE IN BY DAVID WHYTE

Time to Allow	Topics This Could Be Specifically Useful for
Reading time: 5 minutes Reflection time: 15 minutes or more	Exploring resistance Finding your own direction of travel

The poem: "Start close in …"

Start close in,
don't take the second step
or the third,
start with the first
thing
close in,
the step that you don't want to take.

Start with
the ground
you know,
the pale ground
beneath your feet,
your own
way to begin
the conversation.

Start with your own
question,
give up on other
people's questions,
don't let them
smother something
simple.

To hear
another's voice,
follow
your own voice,
wait until
that voice
becomes an
intimate private ear
that can
really listen
to another.

Start right now
take a small step
you can call your own
don't follow
someone else's
heroics, be humble
and focused,
start close in,
don't mistake
that other
for your own.

Start close in,
don't take
the second step
or the third,
start with the first
thing
close in,
the step
you don't want to take.

A pathway for reflection

See pages 161–162.

Why this appealed to me

A few years ago, I attended a salon organised by the Beyond Partnership who had invited David Whyte to share his poetry. I experienced him as a powerful personal presence. His voice, with its lilting Irish tone, was most memorable. While he didn't read this particular poem, I could almost hear him narrate it. The phraseology is distinctively his, and I like the repetition of the opening and closing verses almost coming full circle.

I encountered the poem when getting bookings for a new programme was feeling like an uphill struggle. It prompted the question in me "What is the step that I don't want to take?" I began to notice that I was so busy aspiring for volume take up, I had overlooked what was "close in." When I did so, my first step was to reach out to those already booked to see how we could co-create a solution. Rather than a volume of participants what emerged was a small, intimate and sustainable group. Having "listened to my own voice," I was able to embrace the new format and drown out my perception that only a large cohort would indicate success.

Drawing from my own learning, I offer the poem as a gentle encouragement for us to move forward with what we have.

Reference

Whyte, D. (2019) *David Whyte: Essentials*. USA: Many Rivers Press.

Copyright notice

10 TEACH YOUR CHILDREN BY TED PERRY

Time to Allow	Topics This Could Be Specifically Useful for
Reading time: 3 minutes Reflection time: 15 minutes or more	Interconnectedness between ourselves and our environment Considering what legacy we want to be responsible for Challenging how we come to understand what we perceive as true

The piece

> *If we sell this land to you, I will make now this condition: You must teach your children that the ground beneath their feet responds more lovingly to our steps than to yours, because it is rich with the lives of our kin. Teach your children what we have taught our children that the earth is our mother. Whatever befalls the earth befalls the sons and daughters of the earth. If men spit upon the ground, they spit upon themselves. This we know. The earth does not belong to us; we belong to the earth. This we know. All things are connected like the blood which unites our family. If we kill the snakes, the field mice will multiply and destroy our corn. All things are connected. Whatever befalls the earth, befalls the sons and daughters of the earth. Man did not weave the web of life; he is merely a strand in it. Whatever he does to the web, he does to himself.*

A pathway for reflection

See pages 161–162.

Why this appealed to me

In our current context, we are becoming a society which is more aware of our ecology. I include this piece to deliberately invite us to think about our role in the climate crisis. This piece may be familiar already – it offers a powerful reminder of our interconnectedness with our environment and our duty to educate those around us to live with an appropriate measure of respect.

Most people will associate the words as an excerpt from Chief Seattle's 1854 speech in response to the Governor's proposal of buying the Natives' land. However, I discovered by reading Henry Smith's 1887 transcript of that speech – that it is not there! I then located Eli Gifford's work which identifies how many writers have leveraged Chief Seathl's words. Appendix 7 of Gifford's book provides the original words (used here) and are part of a 1970 screenplay written by Ted Perry for the producer John Stevens and the film "Home." This was an environmentalist movie produced for the Southern Baptist Radio and Television Commission. Delving even further, Ted Perry had not used the original Chief Seathl script, but William Arrowsmith's translation of it from 1969 (Appendix 6 of the Gifford book).

So, in fact, this poem (script) has impacted upon me for many reasons. Despite its chronology, its content feels current and wise. Locating its origin reminds me how rarely we take the time and trouble to check the true origin of what we think we know. Yet when we do, we often uncover a more interesting truth.

Reference

Gifford, E. (1951) *The Many Speeches of Chief Seattle. (Seathl): The Manipulation of the Record on Behalf of Religious, Political and Environmental Causes.* North Charleston, SC: CreateSpace Independent Publishing Platform.

11 THE WAY IT IS BY WILLIAM STAFFORD

Acknowledgements: With thanks to Clare Norman who brought this poem to my attention

Time to Allow	Topics This Could Be Specifically Useful for
Reading time: 5 minutes	Reflecting on purpose, vision, values and beliefs
Reflection time: 15 minutes or more	Questioning direction or identity

The poem: "The way it is"

There's a thread you follow. It goes among
things that change. But it doesn't change.
People wonder about what you are pursuing.
You have to explain about the thread.
But it is hard for others to see.
While you hold it you can't get lost.
Tragedies happen; people get hurt
or die; and you suffer and get old.
Nothing you do can stop time's unfolding.
You don't ever let go of the thread.

A pathway for reflection

See pages 161–162.

Why this appealed to me

I invite participants of my regular reflective practice sessions to share poems that have had an impact for them. This is one of them (thanks Clare!). For me, this poem speaks about the groundedness that arises when an individual has clarity about their values and beliefs or about their purpose and ambition. I like the way the poem recognises that life can be harsh and that one needs a persistence and resilience as we respond to those challenges. It reminds me that when we are connected with our truths – those core elements which make each of us who we are – we are somehow able to find our way in spite of those challenges. I have found it useful to prompt reflection when I am with clients that seem lost or directionless or confused about their identity.

References

Stafford, W. (1994) *The Way It Is. New and Selected Poems.* Minneapolis: Greywolf Publishers.
Credit: William Stafford, "The Way It Is" from Ask Me: 100 Essential Poems. Copyright © 1977, 2004 by William Stafford and the

12 UNTITLED BY ALASTAIR KIDD

Time to Allow	Topics This Could Be Specifically Useful for
Reading time: 5 minutes Reflection time: 15 minutes or more	Exploring the motivation and engagement of clients Understanding what is mobilising the client's self-discovery process

The poem: "Untitled"

I can no longer meet folks in the foothills of leadership.
Journey with me instead to the floor of the high valley.
There we will discover clear sun lit air.

This may be the most exhilarating venture so far.
One that goes through foggy uncharted territory.
We will go with good strength and at a steady pace.
Stilling, tenderness and spaciousness will companion us.
Approaching hard edges with softness.

There will be losses along the way and much to gain,
previously unknown or never thought possible.
We may not know where we are or where we have been
until emerging on the floor of that high valley,
Some distance from where we started
and very close by.

The tall snow-capped mountains
more recognisable and friendly now.
There is magic in this place
and it may feel like magic got us here.

A pathway for reflection

See pages 161–162.

Why this appealed to me

This poem was written by one of my very first supervisees – we stopped working together some years back, but we remain connected on LinkedIn. Earlier this year, he posted this poem and it took me by surprise when I realised it was an original piece! I was struck by his eloquence and his chosen metaphors impacted me deeply.

I am not entirely sure what Alastair intended by the poem. It is interesting that it is "untitled" – but as I read it, I was reminded of his desire to do the very best he could. Which of course is only possible when our clients are ready to do their best too.

As a supervisor, I often meet coaches who are frustrated by the recognition that a client, with huge potential, is not yet ready to fully realise it. For me, the opening of the poem speaks of a practitioner's reluctance to engage with a client who is content with only getting to first camp, because they believe so much more is possible for them.

By contrast, I also experience the exhilaration of coaches when their clients start to reach their peak. As the poem closes, Alastair uses the analogy of magic as a way of describing impactful coaching. I notice my need to clarify that, for me, any magic that exists is not the result of my magic wand, but rather a co-creation generated by two curious souls.

Anecdotes from practitioners

Fire by Judy Brown

What shifted as a result of the exercise?

A powerful reminder that it's important to make space to breathe, pause, reflect and recharge during a busy day and in a life packed full of activities and commitments. Just like the fire in Judy's poem, we need space in our lives to focus on the gaps and "in-betweens" because that is where the oxygen is that will re-energise and sustain us.

How did you feel about the reflective experience?

Reading the poem in the reflective practice session was very timely for me at the start of the year. My natural tendency is to cram so much into my life – this originates partially from my wide range of interests, but mainly because both my parents died in their early 60s and, as a result, my wanting to live life to the max. It's great when everything flows smoothly; however, my busyness can lead to irritability, exhaustion and illness.

The poem would normally have passed me by as I would have skimmed the words, speed reading at pace before my next task. What the reflective practice session provides is an hour dedicated to slowing down and savouring each moment, word, sound and breath – utter bliss

Jo Bond, Reflective Practice Space, 19 January 2022

Liminal Places by Charlotte Housden

What shifted as a result of the exercise?

A move from resistance to acceptance. I had the self-awareness to understand I was in a period of transition, but it felt a lonely place – and somewhere in which I shouldn't be staying for long. As if the space "in-between" was something to resist inhabiting. As a result of the exercise, I felt a shift to an acceptance that being in transition was appropriate. The exercise legitimised the space as a valid and valuable position to live in for a while. I felt able to lose some of the anxiety around the transition and relate to the potential that the liminal place may offer me.

How did you feel about the reflective experience?

I hadn't used a poem in this way before and its impact as the stimulus in the reflective session took me by surprise. The experience provided a healthy release from the daily habit of working. Being with others in the space, yet alone to reflect, felt both supportive and private. The reflective experience has stayed with me and recently, I was working with a group who were signalling anxiety and uncertainty. I provided a space for them to reflect, offering a calm and free-flowing session before we moved onto more content. Had I not experienced reflection in this context myself, I would not have the tools to support others in the moment.

Helen Robson, Reflective Practice Space, June 2022

INDEX

Printed in Great Britain
by Amazon

23498647R00126